Greek Gods and Goddesses Gone Wild: Bad Behavior and Divine Excess From Zeus's Philandering to Dionysus's Benders

By Michael Rank and Alexander Stuart Murray

Table of Contents

Introduction: Gods Behaving Badly............................4

Chapter 1: Born to be Wild – Gods of the Highest Order and the Creation of the World........................11

Chapter 2: Lower Gods and their Low-Down Behavior 56

Chapter 3: Heroes and the Gods who Exploited Them 79

Conclusion: When the Gods are Made in Our Image 139

Excerpt from "History's Most Insane Rulers"........145

Connect With Michael... 152

About the Author...153

Introduction: Gods Behaving Badly

Men create gods after their own image, not only with regard to their form but with regard to their mode of life.

– Aristotle

Why did the Greek gods behave so badly?

A student of mythology quickly notices that Zeus, Hera, Aphrodite, and the rest of the pantheon are not cut from the same mold of the Judeo-Christian God. There is no attempt to make them appear to be perfect, all-knowing, or even good. They act immoral, engage in behaviors such as adultery, revenge, and choosing sides. Many of the half-god/half-human heroes of myth were born due to Zeus philandering with mortal women behind Hera's back. The gods would frequently steal from each other, particularly in the case of Hermes. Petty feuding seemed to be the pastime on Mount Olympos. And Homer's epic "The Iliad" is essentially a story of the gods pitting members of the Trojan and the Greek armies against each other in history's most epic chess match.

The brusqueness of their behavior appears shocking to a monotheistic audience. Judaism, Christianity, and Islam each claim that the fundamental character of God is perfection.

Thousands of apologetic books have been written to defend against accusations of imperfections in their character that skeptics bring up ("Why does God permit the existence of evil?"). However, the behavior of Zeus and the other Hellenistic deities would not have been shocking to an ancient Greek audience. They did not think of their gods as omniscient or omnipotent. While they were immortal and more powerful than humans, it was not on an infinite scale. Rather, the chief characteristic that earned worship from ancient Greeks was their power. Ares held the power of battle, Aphrodite held the power of love and attraction, and Artemis held the power of a successful hunt, along with the ability to hold back or bring about a plague. But despite their power, they were quite interested in pretending to be human and mingling among us. Cameo appearances by the gods populated the Trojan war, and many people found themselves cursed by accidentally insulting a god in human flesh.

These gods were not given human attributes because ancient Greeks wanted to make a mockery of the entire religious enterprise; it was a way to give divine character to the natural world they lived in. This was a time when all but the most wealthy members of society worked in agricultural-related professions and lived and died according to their environmental conditions. When Greek mythology developed, particularly in Homer's epic poetry in 800 B.C., Socrates, Plato, and Aristotle had not yet systematized philosophy to provide a means of logically understanding the world. Scientific explanations for fires, floods, earthquakes, and famines did not exist; therefore an explanation based on the displeasure of the gods would have to do. This was done because the Greeks hoped that they could then influence natural events by appeasing the god that controlled the event in question. Was there a poor catch of fish? Pray to Poseidon that he may bring you a large haul. Did a fair Greek maiden not respond to the sonnets that you penned for her about her articulated eye brows and freckled complexion that resembles the Peloponnese rocky soil? Ask Aphrodite to change her heart and warm up to your prose. Is the city in need of feasting and revelry to cheer up its mood? Beseech Dionysus to bring a party atmosphere and possibly some of his vintage wine.

This book will look at the acts of the gods from Greek mythology and explain why they were so human in what they did. It organizes the most famous and infamous stories known in the Hellenistic mythological tradition. Much of the information found here comes from Alexander Stuart Murray's "Manual of Mythology" a classic compendium of ancient mythological myths that was originally published in London in 1874. I have edited the original work and revised, updated, and appended it to make it a more lively read. It is broken up into sections devoted to the different parts of the mythological pantheon. We will start with the creation myth, then deities of the highest order, followed by lower-order deities, and finishing with demigods and heroes. The original book focused on the myths from Greek, Roman, Norse, Old German, Hindu, and Egyptian culture. In this edited version I have decided to eliminate the non-Greek myths since they are less well known the reader. If you are interested in reading about these other cultures, you can download a free ebook featuring them at http://michaelrank.net/freebook.

Greek gods were all-too-human and intimately connected with nature because everywhere in nature was felt the presence of invisible beings: in the sky, with its luminaries and clouds; on the sea, with its fickle, changeful movements; on the earth, with its lofty peaks, its plains and rivers. It seemed that man himself, and everything around him, was upheld by divine power; that his career was marked out for him by a rigid fate that even the gods could not alter, should they wish it on occasion. He was indeed free to act, but the consequences of all his actions were settled beforehand.

These deities to whom the affairs of the world were entrusted were, it was believed, immortal, though not eternal in their existence, as we shall see when we come to read the legends concerning their birth. In Crete there was even a story of the Zeus's death, his tomb being pointed out; and, further, the fact that the gods were believed to sustain their existence by means of nectar and ambrosia, is sufficient proof that they could be susceptible to old age. Being immortal, they were next, as a consequence, supposed to be omnipotent and omniscient. Their physical strength was extraordinary, the earth shaking sometimes under their movement. Whatever they did was done speedily. They moved through space almost without the loss of a moment of time. They knew all things, saw and heard all things with rare exceptions. They were wise, and communicated their wisdom to men. They had a most strict sense of justice, punished crime rigorously, and rewarded noble actions, though it is true that they were less conspicuous for the latter. Their punishments came quickly, as a rule; but even if late, even if not till the second generation, still they came without fail. The sinner who escaped retribution in this life was sure to obtain it in the lower world; while the good who died unrewarded enjoyed the fruit of their good actions in the next life.

To many this did not appear a satisfactory way of managing human affairs, and hence there frequently arose doubts as to the absolute justice of the gods, and even the sanctity of their lives. These doubts were reflected in stories, which, to the indignation of men like the poet Pindar, represented this or that one of the gods as guilty of some offense or other, such as they were believed to punish. Philosophers endeavored to explain these stories, some as mere fictions of the brain, others as allegories under which lay a profound meaning. But the mass of the people accepted them as they came, and nevertheless believed in the perfect sanctity of the gods – even when their shameful behavior indicated the exact opposite – being satisfied that human wickedness was detested and punished by them.

Most of all, the gods loved to meddle. There

were tales of personal visits and adventures of the gods among men, taking part in battles, and appearing in dreams. They were conceived to possess the form of human beings, and to be, like men, subject to love and pain, but always characterized by the highest qualities and grandest form that could be imagined. To produce statues of them that would equal this high ideal was the chief ambition of artists; and in presence of statues in which such success had been attained, the popular mind felt an awe as if in some way the deity were near.

Over time Greek society came to understand that their gods had less than savory aspects. This became particularly clear as Christianity spread and their ancient beliefs no longer had a monopoly in the marketplace of ideas. In later times of higher civilization and greater refinement, when the origin of the gods as personifications of natural phenomena was lost sight of, many of these stories came to be viewed as disgraceful, and by being made the subject of public ridicule in plays tended largely to uproot the general faith in the gods. Philosophers attempted to explain them as allegories. Others, who did not themselves believe them, advised that the popular faith in them should not be disturbed.

But we who live in other times, having no need of a religion that has long since passed away, and desiring only to trace its origin and the source of its long and deep influence on a great nation, may look at them in a more objective manner mood. Without any further ado, let us look at the un-godlike behavior of the greatest figures in Greek mythology.

Chapter 1: Born to be Wild – Gods of the Highest Order and the Creation of the World

The ancient Greeks believed in making something out of nothing. This was their approach to the origin of the universe, that it appeared *ex nihilio*. From then on the creation account reads like the book of Genesis: In the beginning the world was a great shapeless mass or chaos, out of which was fashioned first the spirit of love, Eros, and the broad-chested earth, Gaea; then Erebos, darkness, and Nyx, night. From a union of the two latter sprang Ether, the clear sky, and Hemera, day. The earth, by virtue of the power by which it was fashioned, produced in turn, Uranos.

Eros, the oldest and at the same time the youngest of the gods, decided to pair off the elements of the earth and acted as something of a celestial matchmaker. First in importance of these pairs were Uranos and Gaea, heaven and earth, who filled the earth with a host of beings, Titans, Giants, and Cyclops, of far greater physical frame and energy than the races who succeeded them. It was a nice poetic idea – that through a divine love making order was brought out of chaos and opposite things were brought together. But soon an avalanche of unintended consequences followed.

The Gods lived on Mount Olympos, and for that reason were styled the Olympian deities, twelve in number: Zeus, Hera, Poseidon, Demeter, Apollo, Artemis, Hephaeslos, Athena, Aeres, Aphrodite, Hermes, and Hestia. Though allied to each other by various degrees of relationship, and worshipped in many places at altars dedicated to them as a united body, they did not always act together in harmony, or rarely did so. An early example of this is Zeus challenging the other gods to a celestial game of tug-of-war. Zeus threatened to hurl the others into Tartaros, and challenged them to move him from Olympos by letting themselves down with a golden chain and pulling with all their might. Should they try it, he said, he could easily draw them up with earth and sea to the bargain, fasten the chain to the top of Olympos, and let the whole hang in mid air.

The race of the gods began with Uranos, the personification of the sky as the ancients saw and understood its phenomena. Next succeeded Kronos, and lastly, Zeus. The *pater familias* of the gods decided to kick off their race with a bad start. He immediately engaged in incest with his mother and produced a number of offspring with more defects than an Appalachian clan. Uranos was a son of Gaea, whom he afterwards married. Although the Greeks did not know of genetics and the dangers of inbreeding, they got their mythology right in that the fruit of this Oedipal union was a bit rotten. They produced the Titans, the Hekatoncheires, and the Cyclops.

The Hekatoncheires, or Centimani, were beings each with a hundred hands. They were three in number: Kottos, Gyges or Gyes, and

Briareus, and represented the frightful crashing of waves and its resemblance to the convulsion of earthquakes. The Cyclops also were three in number: Brontes with his thunder, Steropes with his lightning, and Arges with his stream of light. They were represented as having only one eye, which was placed between nose and brow. It was, however, a large flashing eye, as became beings who were personifications of the storm-cloud, with its flashes of destructive lightning and peals of thunder. From a similarity observed between the phenomena of storms and those of volcanic eruptions, it was usually supposed that the Cyclops lived in the heart of burning mountains, above all, in Mount Etna, in Sicily, where they acted as apprentices of Hephaestos, assisting him to make thunderbolts for Zeus, and in other works. Uranos realized that his offspring called into question the entire idea of mother-son couplings. He was alarmed at their promise of fierceness and strength and did what any responsible parent of inbred offspring did. He cast the Hekatoncheires and Cyclops at their birth back into the womb of the earth from which they had sprung.

The Titans were, like the Olympian deities, twelve in number, and grouped for the most part in pairs: Okeanos and Tethys, Hyperion and Theia, Kreios and Eurybia, Koios and Phoebe, Kronosand Rhea, Japetos and Themis. Their names, though not in every case quite intelligible, show that they were personifications of those primary elements and forces of nature to the operations of which, in the first ages, the present configuration of the earth was supposed to be due. This explains why the mythologizers were not shy in attributing less-than-savory aspects to their character. While Themis, Mnemosyne, and Japetos may be singled out as personifications of a civilizing force in the nature of things, and as conspicuous for having offspring endowed with the same character, the other Titans appear to represent wild, powerful, and obstructive forces. In keeping with this character we find them rising in rebellion first against their father and afterwards against Zeus.

Family infighting soon became more common in the Greek pantheon than daytime talk shows. In the former experiment the result was that Uranos threw them into Tartaros, where he kept them bound. But Gaea grieving at the hard fate of her offspring, provided the youngest son, Kronos, with a sickle or curved knife, which she had made of stubborn adamant, and told him how and when to wound his father with it irremediably. The enterprise succeeded, the Titans were set free, married their sisters (taking a cue from mom and dad), and begat a numerous family of divine beings, while others of the same class sprang from the blood of the wound of Uranos as it fell to the ground. Of these were the Giants, monsters with legs formed of serpents; the Melian nymphs, or nymphs of the oaks, from which the shafts used in war were fashioned; and the Erinys, or Furiae, as the Romans called them, Tisiphone, Megaera, and Alekto, creatures whose function it was originally to avenge the shedding of a parent's blood. Their form was that of women, with hair of snakes and girdles of vipers. They were a terror to criminals, whom they pursued with unrelenting fury.

Keeping relations in the family continued and they became even more bizarre, as the practice of *eating ones own children* began. Uranos, deposed from the throne of the gods, was succeeded by Kronos, who married his own sister Rhea, a daughter of Gaea, who bore him Pluto, Poseidon, and Zeus, Hestia, Demeter, and Hera. To prevent the fulfillment of a prophecy which had been communicated to him by his parents, that, like his father, he too would be dethroned by his youngest born, Kronos swallowed his first five children apparently as each came into the world. But when the sixth child appeared, Rhea, his wife, determined to save it, and succeeded in duping her husband by giving him a stone (perhaps rudely hewn into the figure of an infant) wrapped in swaddling clothes, which he swallowed, believing he had got rid of another danger.

While the husband was being deceived in this fashion, Zeus, the newly born child, was conveyed to the island of Crete, and there concealed in a cave on Mount Ida. The nymphs Adrastea and Ida tended and nursed him, the goat Amalthea supplied him with milk, bees gathered honey for him, and in the meantime, lest his infantile cries should reach the ears of Kronos, Rhea's servants, the Kuretes, were appointed to keep up a continual noise and din in the neighbourhood by dancing and clashing their swords and shields.

But since the ingested children were gods, they managed to survive while living in their father's intestinal tract. When Zeus had grown to manhood he succeeded by the aid of Gaea in persuading Kronos to yield back into the light the sons whom he had swallowed and the stone which had been given him in deceit. The stone was placed at Delphi as a memorial for all time. The liberated gods joined their brethren in a league to drive their father from the throne and set Zeus in his place. This was done; but the change of government, though acquiesced in by the principal deities, was not to be brooked by the Titans, who with the exception of Okeanos proceeded to war.

The seat of war was Thessaly, with its wild natural features suggestive of a conflict in which huge rocks had been torn from mountainsides and shattered by the violence with which they had been thrown in combat. The party of Zeus had its position on Mount Olympos, the Titans on Mount Othrys. The struggle lasted many years, all the might which the Olympians could bring to bear being useless until, on the advice of Gaea, Zeus set free the Cyclops and Hekatoncheires, of whom the former fashioned thunderbolts for him, while the latter advanced on his side with force equal to the shock of an earthquake. The earth trembled down to lowest Tartaros as Zeus now appeared with his terrible weapons and new allies. Old Chaos thought his hour had come, as from a continuous blaze of thunderbolts the earth took fire and the waters seethed in the sea. The rebels were partly slain or consumed, and partly hurled into deep chasms, with rocks and hills reeling after them, and consigning them to a life beneath the surface of the earth. The cause of Kronos was thus lost forever, and the right of Zeus to rule established for all time.

As Uranos, the representative of the fertilizing force in nature, was superseded by Kronos the representative of a ripening force, so Gaea, the primitive goddess of the earth with its productive plains gave way to Rhea, a goddess of the earth with its mountains and forests. Gaea had been the mother of the powerful Titans. Rhea was the mother of gods less given to feats of strength, but more highly gifted: Pluto, Poseidon, and Zeus, Hera, Demeter, and Hestia.

The lofty hills of Asia Minor, while sheltering on their cavernous sides wild animals, such as the panther and lion, which it was Rhea's delight to tame, also looked down on many flourishing cities that it was her duty to protect. In this latter capacity she wore a mural crown, and was styled Mater turrita. But though herself identified with peaceful civilization, that did not keep her from wanting her worshippers to act like revelers at Mardi Gras.

Her worship was always distinguished by wild and fantastic excitement, her priests and devotees rushing through the woods at night with torches burning, maiming and wounding each other, and producing all the din that was possible from the clashing of cymbals, the shrill notes of pipes, and the frantic voice of song. This form of worship stems from the long jealous streak that she had. To account for this peculiarity of her worship, which must have been intended to commemorate some great sorrow, the story was told of how she had loved the young Phrygian shepherd, Attis, whose extraordinary beauty had also won the heart of the king's daughter of Pessinus; how he was destined to marry the princess, and how the goddess, suddenly appearing, spread terror and consternation among the marriage guests Attis escaped to the mountains, maimed himself, and died beside a pine tree, into which his soul transmigrated, while from his blood sprang violets like a wreath round the tree. The goddess implored Zeus to restore her lover. This could not be. But so much was granted that his body should never decay, that his hair should always grow, and that his little finger should always move. The pine was a symbol of winter and sadness, the violet of spring and its hopeful beauty.

Zeus

Zeus was styled the father of gods and men, the ruler and preserver of the world. He was believed to be possessed of every form of power, endued with wisdom, and in his dominion over the human race partial to justice, and with no limit to his goodness and love. However, many other narratives represent him as laboring under human weaknesses and error, particularly for being a serial monogamist, not to mention another god that would gladly devour his children if it meant that he could remain in power. The first wife of Zeus was Metis, a daughter of the friendly Titan Okeanos. But as Fate, a dark and omniscient being, had predicted that Metis would bear Zeus a son who should surpass his father in power, Zeus followed in a manner the example of his father Kronos, by swallowing Metis before she was delivered of her child, and then from his own head gave birth to the goddess of wisdom, Pallas Athena. Next he married, it is said, but only for a time, Themis, and became the father of Astraea and the Horae. His chief love was, however, always for Hera, with her many charms, who, after withstanding his entreaties for a time, at length gave way, and the divine marriage took place amid great rejoicing, not on the part of the gods of heaven alone, for those other deities also, to whom the management of the world had been in various departments delegated, had been invited, and went gladly to the splendid ceremony. Much to Hera's chagrin, however, she would find that Zeus couldn't resist the desire to go tomcatting.

For a while the gods settled down and things went well on earth. These wars over, there succeeded a period that was called the Silver Age. Men were rich then, as in the Golden Age under the rule of Kronos, and lived in plenty; but still they wanted the innocence and contentment which were the true sources of human happiness in the former age; and, accordingly, while living in luxury and delicacy, they became overbearing in their manners to the highest degree, were never satisfied, and forgot the gods, to whom, in their confidence of prosperity and comfort, they denied the reverence they owed. The gods were above all things jealous for worship, and this neglect did not go unnoticed. To punish them, and as a warning against such habits, Zeus swept them away, and concealed them under the earth, where they continued to live as daemons or spirits — not so powerful as the spirits of the men of the Golden Age, but yet respected by those who came after them.

Then came the Bronze Age, a period of constant quarreling and deeds of violence. Instead of cultivated lands and a life of peaceful occupations and orderly habits, there came a day when everywhere might was right; and men, big and powerful as they were, became physically worn out, and sank into the lower world without leaving a trace, and without a claim to a future spiritual life.

Finally came the Iron Age, the age in which most of the best-known mythology stories take place. At this time enfeebled mankind had to toil for bread with their hands, and, bent on gain, did their best to overreach each other. Dike or Astraea, the goddess of justice and good faith, modesty and truth, turned her back on such scenes, and retired to Olympos. Zeus determined to destroy the human race by a great flood. The whole of Greece lay under water, and none but Deukalion and his wife Pyrrha were saved. Leaving the summit of Parnassos, where they had escaped the flood, they were commanded by the gods to become the founders of a new race of men — that is, the present race. To this end, it is said they cast around them as they advanced stones, which presently assumed the forms of men, who, when the flood had quite disappeared, commenced to cultivate the land again and spread themselves in all directions; but being little better than the race that had been destroyed, they, too, often drew down the displeasure of Zeus and suffered at his hands. Gaining his displeasure was never hard, as the Greeks would soon find out.

Hera

Greeks ascribed male and female attributes to nature, both the good and bad characteristics of men and women. Hence, mythology was something of an ancient "Men are from Mars, Women are from Venus" storybook, with all of Zeus and Hera's marriage quarrels spilling out from Olympus and into the world. Hera was a divine personification of what may be called the female power of the heavens — that is, the atmosphere, with its fickle and yet fertilizing properties; while Zeus represented those properties of the heavens that appeared to be of a male order. To their marriage was traced all the blessings of nature, and when they met, as on Mount Ida in a golden cloud, sweet fragrant flowers sprang up around them. A tree with golden apples grew up at their marriage feast, and streams of ambrosia flowed past their couch in the happy island of the west. That marriage ceremony took place, it was believed, in spring, and to keep up a recollection of it, an annual festival was held at that season in her honor.

Hera was considered to be the personification of a thunderstorm. Like the sudden and violent storms, however, which in certain seasons break the peacefulness of the sky of Greece, the meetings of this divine pair often resulted in temporary quarrels and wrangling, the blame of which was usually traced to Hera; poets, and most of all Homer, in the Iliad, describing her as frequently jealous, angry, and quarrelsome, her character as lofty and proud, cold, and not free from bitterness, Of these scenes of discord we have several instances, as when (Iliad i. 586) Zeus actually beat her, and threw her son Hephaestos out of Olympos; or when, vexed at her plotting against Hercules, he hung her out of Olympos with two great weights (earth and sea) attached to her feet, and her arms bound by golden fetters; or again when Hera, with Poseidon and Athena, attempted to chain down Zeus, and would have succeeded had not Thetis brought to his aid the sea giant Aegaeon. As goddess of storms, Hera was consistently described as the mother of Ares, herself taking part in war occasionally, as against the Trojans, and enjoying the honor of festivals, accompanied by warlike contests, as at Argos, where the prize was a sacred shield.

The character, however, in which Hera was most generally viewed was that of queen of heaven, and as the faithful wife of Zeus claiming the highest conceivable respect and honor.

Herself the ideal of womanly virtues, she made it a principal duty to protect them among mortals, punishing with severity all trespassers against her moral law — but, naturally, none so much as those who had been objects of her husband's affections—as, for instance, Semele, the mother of Dionysos, or Alkmene, the mother of Hercules. Her worship was restricted for the most part to women, who, according to the various stages of womanhood, regarded her in a different light: some as a bride, styling her Parthenia; others as a wife, with the title of Gamelia, Zygia or Teleia; and others again in the character of Eileithyia, as helpful at child-birth. But her chief attribute was jealousy. As queen of heaven and wife of Zeus she will be found, in connection with the legends of Argos and its neighbourhood, possessed, from motives of jealousy, of a hatred towards the nocturnal phenomena of the sky, and especially the moon, as personified by the wandering Io, whom she placed under the surveillance of Argos, a being with innumerable eyes, and apparently a personification of the starry system.

It has already been told how, when all the resources had failed which the Titans could bring to bear for the restoration of Kronos to the throne, the government of the world was divided by lot among his three sons, Zeus, Poseidon, and Hades. To Zeus fell, besides a general supremacy, the control of the heavens; and we have seen how he and his consort Hera, representing the phenomena of that region, were conceived as divine persons possessed of a character and performing actions such as were suggested by those phenomena. To Poseidon fell the control of the element of water, and he in like manner was conceived as a god, in whose character and actions were reflected the phenomena of that element, whether as the broad navigable sea, or as the cloud which gives fertility to the earth, growth to the grain and vine, or as the fountain which refreshes man, cattle, and horses.

Poseidon

Land disputes broke out among this family. It was so extreme that gods would destroy lands by sending monsters if they thought that they were not getting their fair share of property. A dispute ending unfavorably for Poseidon was that which he had with Hera concerning the district of Argos. But in this case his indignation took the opposite course of causing a perpetual drought. Other incidents of the same nature were his disputes with Helios for the possession of Corinth, with Zeus for Egina, with Dionysos for Naxos, and with Apollo for Delphi. The most obvious illustrations, however, of the encroaching tendency of the sea are the monsters which Poseidon sent to lay waste coast lands, such as those which Hesione and Andromeda were offered to appease.

Poseidon appeared to water the earth based on his fickle moods and romantic longings. In the Iliad Poseidon appears only in his capacity of ruler of the sea, inhabiting a brilliant palace in its depths, traversing its surface in a chariot, or stirring the powerful billows till the earth shakes as they crash upon the shore. This limitation of his functions, though possibly to be accounted for by the nature of the poem, is remarkable for this reason, that among the earliest myths associated with his worship are those in which he is represented in connection with well-watered plains and valleys. In the neighborhood of Lerna, in the parched district of Argos, he had struck the earth with his trident, and caused three springs to well up for love of Amymone, whom he found in distress, because she could not obtain the water which her father Danaos had sent her to fetch.

In Thessaly a stroke of his trident had broken through the high mountains, which formerly shut in the whole country and caused it to be frequently flooded with water. By that stroke he formed the pleasant vale of Tempe, through which the water collecting from the hills might flow away. A district well supplied with water was favorable to pasture and the rearing of horses, and in this way the horse came to be doubly his symbol, as god of the water of the sea and on the land. In Arcadia, with its mountainous land and fine streams and valleys, he was worshipped side by side with Demeter, with whom, it was believed, he begat that winged and wonderfully fleet horse Arion. In Bœotia, where he was also worshipped, the mother of Arion was said to have been Erinys, to whom he had appeared in the form of a horse. With Medusa he became the father of the winged horse Pegasos, which was watered at springs by Nymphs, and appeared to poets as the symbol of poetic inspiration. And again, as an instance of his double capacity as god of the sea and pasture streams, the ram, with the golden fleece for which the Argonauts sailed, was said to have been his offspring by Theophane, who had been changed into a lamb. Chief among his other offspring were, on the one hand, the giant Antaeos, who derived from his mother Earth a strength which made him invincible, till Hercules lifting him in the air overpowered him, and the Cyclops, Polyphemos; on the other hand, Pelias, who sent out the Argonauts, and Neleus the father of Nestor.

To return to the instances of rebellious conduct on the part of Poseidon, it appears that after the conclusion of the war with the Giants a disagreement arose between him and Zeus, the result of which was that Poseidon was suspended for the period of a year from the control of the sea, and was further obliged during the time to serve, along with Apollo, Laomedon the King of Troy, and to help to build the walls of that city. Some say that the building of the walls was voluntary on the part of both gods, and was done to test the character of Laomedon, who afterwards refused to give Poseidon the reward agreed upon. Angry at this, the god devastated the land by a flood, and sent a sea-monster, to appease which Laomedon was driven to offer his daughter Hesione as a sacrifice. Hercules, however, set the maiden free and slew the monster. Thus defeated, Poseidon relented none of his indignation towards the Trojans, and would have done them much injury in after times, when they were at war with the Greeks, but for the interference of Zeus.

The gods controlled the lives of humans according to their mood, and they controlled their deaths in much the same way. There were generally three places where a human could be sent – the underworld as the abiding place of the great mass of the dead, and two other regions where spirits of the departed were to be found — the one Elysion (the Elysian Fields), with the islands of the blessed, and the other Tartaros. The former region was most commonly placed in the remotest West, and the latter as far below the earth as the heavens are above it. In early times it appears to have been believed that Elysion and the happy islands were reserved less for the virtuous and good than for certain favorites of the gods. There, under the sovereignty of Kronos, they lived again a kind of second golden age of perpetual duration. But in later times there spread more and more the belief in a happy immortality reserved for all the good, and particularly for those who had been initiated into the Eleusinian Mysteries. Tartaros, on the other hand, was the region where those were condemned to punishment who had committed any crime against the gods while on earth. What was the misery of their condition we shall be able to judge from the following account of a few of the best known of those condemned to such punishment — as Tantalos, Ixion, Sisyphos, Tityos, and the Danaïdes.

Tantalos, once a king of Phrygia, had given offense to the gods by his overbearing and treachery, as well as by the cruelty that he had practiced on his own son. For this he was doomed to Tartaros, and there to suffer from an unceasing dread of being crushed by a great rock that hung above his head, he the while standing up to the throat in water, yet possessed of a terrible thirst which he could never quench, and a gnawing hunger which he tried in vain to allay with the tempting fruits that hung over his head but withdrew at every approach he made. It is from his treatment that we get the word "tantalize" in English today.

Ixion, once a sovereign of Thessaly, had, like Tantalos, outraged the gods, and was in consequence sentenced to Tartaros, there to be lashed with serpents to a wheel which a strong wind drove continually round and round.

Sisyphos, once king of Corinth, had by treachery and hostility incurred the anger of the gods in a high degree, and was punished in Tartaros by having to roll a huge stone up a height, which he had no sooner done, by means of his utmost exertion, than it rolled down again. If we are doing something endlessly laborous, such as filling out a pile of paperwork at our desk job, we can refer to this as a Sisyphean ordeal.

Tityos, a giant who once lived in Eubcea, had misused his strength to outrage Leto (the mother of Apollo and Artemis), and was condemned by Zeus to Tartaros, where two enormous vultures gnawed continually his liver, which always grew again.

The Danaides, daughters of Danaos, king of Argos, were sentenced to Tartaros for the

28

murder of their husbands. The punishment prescribed for them was to carry water, and continue to pour it into a broken cistern or vase, the labor being all in vain, and going on for ever.

It is interesting to note that of all the punishments that the gods could have inflicted on those for breaking their commands, they chose a meaningless task. Instead of physical punishment, torture, or condemnation that is an ironic turn of events often found in Dante's Inferno (such as those who committed suicide being denied their human form because they destroyed their own mortal body), the gods chose boredom. Albert Camus insightfully noted this phenomenon: "The gods had condemned Sisyphus to ceaselessly rolling a rock to the top of a mountain, whence the stone would fall back of its own weight. They had thought with some reason that there is no more dreadful punishment than futile and hopeless labor."

Demeter

Returning back to earth, we see in the character of Demeter, goddess of agriculture, that she inflicted much misery on those whose job was to work on the earth itself. In turn, she was the victim of other gods who behaved like a jealous ex-boyfriend issued a restraining order. In Arcadia, Crete, and Samothrace we find her associated with a mythical hero called Jasion, reputed to have been the first sower of grain, to whom she bore a child, whose name of Plutos shows him to be a personification of the wealth derived from the cultivation of grain. In Thessaly there was a legend of her hostility to a hero sometimes called Erysichton, 'the earth upturner' or 'the ploughman,' and sometimes Aethon, a personification of famine. Again we find a reference to her function as goddess of agriculture in the story that once, when Poseidon threatened with his superior strength to mishandle her, Demeter took the form of a horse and fled from him; but the god, taking the same shape, pursued and overtook her. She was apparently obligated to bear him a child by losing this divine horse race. The result was that she afterwards bore him Arion, a wonderful black horse of incredible speed, and gifted with intelligence and speech like a man. Pain and shame at the birth of such a creature drove her to hide for a long time in a cave, till at last she was purified by a bath in the river Ladon, and again appeared among the other deities. From the necessities of agriculture originated the custom of living in settled communities. It was Demeter who first inspired mankind with an interest in property and the ownership of land, who created the feeling of patriotism and the maintenance of law and order.

As a testimony to her capriciousness, Greeks chose to honor her by engaging in orgies. The next phase of her character was that which came into prominence at harvest time, when the bare stubble fields reminded her worshippers of the loss of her daughter Persephone. At that time two kinds of festivals were held in her honor, the one kind called Haloa or Thalysia, being apparently mere harvest festivals, the other called Thesmophoria. Of the latter, as conducted in the village of Halimus in Attica, we know that it was held from the 9th to the 13th of October each year, that it could only be participated in by married women, that at one stage of the proceedings Demeter was hailed as the mother of the beautiful child, and that this joy afterwards gave way to expressions of the deepest grief at her loss of her daughter. At night orgies were held at which mysterious ceremonies were mixed with boisterous amusement of all sorts.

Hephaestos

Another god who was an anthropomorphism of an element was Hephaestos, the divine personification of the fire that burns within the earth and bursts forth in volcanic eruptions — fire which has no connection with the sun or the lightning of heaven; and such being his character, we can readily understand the mutual dislike which existed between him and the god of the light of heaven. He was indeed the son of Zeus and Hera, the supreme deities of heaven; but he was born to be a cause of quarrel between them, and alternately at enmity with both. Once, when he took his mother's part, Zeus seized him by the heels and tossed him out of Olympos (Iliad i. 560). Through the air he fell for one whole day; at evening, as the sun went down, reaching the island of Lemnos, where he was found by some Sintian people, and taken under friendly care. The place where he was found, and where in after times was the principal centre of his worship, was the neighborhood of the burning mountain Mosychlos.

Hephaestos did not exactly have a loving upbringing. Another version of the myth has it that Hera, ashamed of the decrepit form which he presented at his birth, threw him with her own hands from Olympos. Falling into the sea, he was picked up by Thetis and Eurynome, was cared for by them, remained for nine years in the abode of the sea-gods, none but they knowing his whereabouts, and executed there many wonderfully clever examples of handiwork. It may be that this belief originated in observing the nearness of volcanic mountains to the seashore, and the fact of whole islands, like the modern Santorin, being suddenly thrown up from the sea by volcanic force.

He would soon get his revenge on mom for her exiling him. Among the works which he fashioned in the palace of the sea-gods was a cunningly devised throne, which he presented to Hera, as a punishment for casting him out of heaven, knowing that when she sat down on it she would be locked within its secret chains so firmly that no power but his could free her. This happened, and Ares went to bring him by force to her assistance, but was compelled to retreat in fear of the fire brand with which Hephaestos assailed him. At last Dionysos, the god of wine, succeeded by his soft conciliatory speech in restoring friendship between mother and son, and her bonds were forthwith undone. Perhaps it is from this intimacy with Dionysos that he is said to have once appeared as cup-bearer in Olympos, on which occasion the assembled deities could not contain themselves with laughter at the droll figure limping from couch to couch. It seems to be the unsteady flicker of flame that is represented in the lameness of the fire-god, and it may have been the genial influence of the hearth which was the source of the quaint stories about him.

Like his family, Hephaestos was jealous, particularly of anyone who would try to rob him of his fire. As a result, Prometheus would pay dearly for his theft. His worship was traceable back to the earliest times, Lemnos being always the place most sacred to him. There, at the foot of the burning mountain Mosychlos, which is now extinct, stood a very ancient temple of the god — on the very spot, it was said, where Prometheus stole the heavenly fire, and for the theft was taken away among the Caucasus mountains, there nailed alive to a rock by Hephaestos, and compelled to suffer every day an eagle sent by Zeus to gnaw his liver, which daily grew afresh. Citizens of the island knew this story and took measures not to suffer the same fate. A somewhat gloomy ceremony of expiating this theft of fire took place annually in the island, all fires being put out, and forbidden to be relit until the return of the ship that had been despatched to the sacred island of Delos to fetch new fire. Then, after being nine days extinguished, all the fires in dwelling-houses and in workshops were rekindled by the new flame.

Aphrodite

We now turn our attention to Aphrodite, the goddess of love. While we would not expect anything bad out of her – just poetry, love potions, and romantic feelings – she was also credited with all forms of romantic jealousy, which could be one of the nastiest emotions of all. Accordingly we find in her character, side by side with what is beautiful and noble, much that is coarse and unworthy. In the best times of Greece the refined and beautiful features of her worship were kept in prominence, both in poetry and art; but these, when times of luxury succeeded, had to give way to impurities of many kinds.

She also had quite an entourage. The earlier and pure Greek phase of her character, in which she is called a daughter of Zeus and Dione, was that of a goddess who presides over human love; she is described as accompanied by her son Eros (Armor or Cupid), the Charites (Graces), the Horse, Himeros (God of the desire of love), Pothos (God of the anxieties of love), and Peitho (Suadela, or the soft speech of love). Despite all her grandeur, she liked to go slumming in the Greek countryside and would not take 'no' for an answer, even if the object of her affections had died. Her special favorite was the young rosy shepherd Adonis; her grief at his death, which was caused by a wild boar, being so great that she would not allow the lifeless body to be taken from her arms until the gods consoled her by decreeing that her lover might continue to live half the year, during the spring and summer, on the earth, while she might spend the other half with him in the lower world, beside Persephone; a reference to the change of seasons, which finds its explanation in the fact of Aphrodite being also goddess of gardens and flowers.

Seasons of the year were even ordered around Aphrodite's romantic moods. Her presence in nature was felt in spring, her absence in winter. This change of the seasons was further observed and celebrated by a festival in honor of Adonis, in the course of which a figure of him was produced, and the ceremony of burial, with weeping and songs of wailing, gone through; after which a joyful shout was raised, "Adonis lives, and is risen again!" She was called Adonaia and Adonias, with reference to this love passage. Next to him her chief favorite was Anchises, to whom she bore Aeneas, who through his son Ascanius, or Julus, became, as story goes, the founder of the great Julian family in Rome. With regard to the story of Pygmalion, the Adonis of Cyprus, into whose statue of her she breathed life on the occasion of one of her festivals, perhaps the same meaning is intended to be conveyed as in the alternate life and death of Adonis — that is, the alternate fervor and coldness of love, or the alternate bloom and frost of nature.

But if she had favors for some she had strong antipathies for others, and proved this spirit on Hippolytos, whom she slew; on Polyphonte, whom she changed into an owl; on Arsinoe whom she turned to stone; and Myrrha, whom she transformed into a myrtle tree. Of her strife and competition with Hera and Athena for the prize of beauty, which the Trojan prince, Paris, awarded to her, we shall give an account later on, in connection with the narrative of the Trojan war.

Athena

Athena's life could not have gone in a normal direction if she wanted due to the strange circumstances of her birth. She is usually described as having sprung into life, fully armed, from the head of Zeus, with its thick black locks, all heaven and earth shaking, while the sea tossing in great billows, and the light of day being extinguished. Zeus, it was said, had previously swallowed his wife Metis, to prevent her giving birth to a son. No being connected with the earth, whether deity or mortal, had a part in her birth. She was altogether the issue only of her father, the god of heaven, who, as the myth very plainly characterizes it, brought her into being out of the black tempest-cloud, and amidst the roar and crash of a storm. Her character must therefore be regarded as forming in some way a complement to his and was very stormy as a result. The purpose for which she was brought into existence must have been that she might do what he would plan, but as the supreme and impartial god, could not carry out. She is at once fearful and powerful as a storm, and, in turn, gentle and pure as the warmth of the sky when a storm has sunk to rest and an air of new life moves over the freshened fields.

She wasn't to be messed with, and many paid the price for not heeding this warning.

To express both these sides of her character — terrible and mighty as compared with open, gentle, and pure — she had the double name of Pallas-Athena: the former was applied to her function of goddess of storms — she who carried the storm-shield of her father. And further, as Pallas, she became the goddess of battle — valiant, conquering, frightening with the sight of her aegis whole crowds of heroes when they vexed her, and even driving Ares before her with her lightning spear. At the same time the soft, gentle, and heavenly side of her character took from her functions, as goddess of battle, that desire of confused slaughter and massacre which distinguished Ares, and formed the contrast we have already mentioned between the two deities of war. Pallas presides over battles, but only to lead on to victory, and through victory, to peace and prosperity.

When the war has been fought out, and that peace established which is always the result of conflict and war, then it is that the goddess Athena reigns in all gentleness and purity, teaching mankind to enjoy peace, and instructing them in all that gives beauty to human life.

These two opposing sides to her character, however, made it hard to enter into a relationship with her. As a result, Athena is represented in the myths as for ever remaining a virgin, scorning the affections which are said to have been frequently offered to her. However, mythologizers considered this an asset instead of a liability, as she was not prone to act irrationally over being jilted by a lover as the other gods were. Instead of suggesting her liability, in the smallest degree, to earthly passions and foibles, the myth shows admirably that she was a divine personification of mind, always unfettered in its movements; a personification, at the same time, of the origin of mind from the brain of the supreme Divine Being: a proof that mind is neither of a male nor of a female order, but a single and independent power at work throughout the whole of nature.

Athena was quite a warrior as well. Single-handed she overpowered the terrible giant Enkelados; but when Zeus' rule was at last firmly established, she took up the task of assisting and protecting those heroes on earth whom she found engaged in destroying the grim creatures and monsters upon it. In this capacity she was the constant friend of Hercules in all his hardships and adventures and of Perseus, whom she helped to slay the Gorgon Medusa, whose head she afterwards wore upon her aegis, and for this reason obtained the name of Gorgophone, or Gorgon slayer. Along with Hera she protected the Argonauts, while to her assistance was due the success with which Theseus overcame and slew monsters of all kinds. She stood by the Greeks in their war against Troy and devised the scheme by which, after ten years' duration, it was brought to a close.

As a result, she is one of the few gods that is presented in an almost completely positive light.

In times of peace, her power as goddess in all kinds of skill and handicraft, of clearness like that of the sky, and of mental activity, was uniformly exercised, as has been said, for the general good and prosperity. The arts of spinning and weaving were described as of her invention. She taught how to tend and nurse newly-born infants; and even the healing art was traced back to her among other gods. The flute, too, was her invention. As became the goddess of war, it was her duty to instruct men in the art of taming horses, of bridling and yoking them to the war-chariot; and in the story of Erichthonios, at Athens, the first mortal who learned from her how to harness horses to chariots. In a word, she was the protectress of all persons employed in art and industry, of those whose business it was on earth to instruct and educate mankind, and therefore to help forward the general happiness.

In works of art Athena generally appears as a virgin of serious aspect, armed with helmet, shield, and spear, wearing long full drapery, and on her breast the aegis, with a border of snakes, and the face of Medusa in the centre. She is often accompanied by an owl. Of the many statues of her; the two most famous in antiquity as works of art were those by the sculptor Pheidias: the one of gold and ivory stood in her great temple at Athens, the Parthenon.

Apollo

It would not be hard for the god of the sun to let such a prestigious title go to his head. From the sun comes our physical light, but that light is at the same time an emblem of all mental illumination, of knowledge, truth, and right, of all moral purity; and in this respect a distinction was made between it as a mental and a physical phenomenon — a distinction which placed Apollo on one side and Helios on the other. Accordingly Apollo is the oracular god who throws light on the dark ways of the future, who slays the Python, that monster of darkness, which made the oracle at Delphi inaccessible. He is the god of music and songs, which are only heard where light and security reign, and the possession of herds is free from danger. Helios, on the other hand, is the physical phenomenon of light, the orb of the sun, which, summer and winter, rises and sets in the sky. His power-bringing secrets to light has been already seen in the story of Vulcan and Venus.

The myth of Apollo is, like that of Aphrodite, one of the oldest in the Greek system, but, unlike the latter, which is at least partly traceable to oriental influence, is a pure growth of the Greek mind. No doubt certain oriental nations had deities of the sun and of light similar in some points to Apollo, but this only proves the simple fact that they viewed the movements of the sun and the operations of light in a general way similarly to the Greeks. We have seen in the preceding chapters how the sky, earth, sea, and lower world were personified by divine beings of a high order, while in the same way other forces and powers in nature were imagined as beings. In the myth of Apollo we shall find represented the various operations of the eternal light of the sun.

Apollo considered the earth his own personal archery range. It is the sun's rays, or the arrows of Apollo, that everywhere, as the fields and gardens teach us, quicken life, and foster it towards ripeness; through them a new life springs all around,and in the warmth of their soft, kindly light the jubilant voice of nature is heard and awakens an echo in the human soul. At the same time these arrows destroy the life of plants and animals ; even man falls under them in southern climates, such as Greece. Their light penetrates to dark corners, and is capable of reaching to inmost recesses. All these ideas are represented in the myth of Apollo, who is therefore conceived in various ways corresponding to the genial radiance of the sun, with all its friendly influences : (i) as the personification of youth and beauty; (2) as god of earthly blessings; (3) as god of the herds that graze on the fields which are warmed by him — a character in which he appeared herding the cattle of Laomedon, which multiplied largely under his care, and when alone piping on his flute, till the wild beasts were attracted from their dens; (4) as god of medicine, who provided for the growth of healing plants; (5) as god of music, for everywhere were heard happy, joyful sounds, when his kindly beams spread light and warmth over nature; (6) as god of oracles which reveal the secrets of the future, as the light of heaven dispels all darkness, and detests nocturnal gloom.

Apollo started out life as the product of a deadbeat mother who had played the part of a divine homewrecker. The story of the birth of Apollo is that he, with his twin sister Artemis, was a son of Zeus and Leto; that Leto, after wandering long hither and thither, pursued by the jealous Hera, at last found shelter in the island of Delos, in the Aegean sea, and there was delivered. It was said that hitherto that island had been only a waste rock driven about in the sea, but that it became fixed in its present position on the occasion of the birth of Apollo and Artemis, an event which was celebrated by a blaze of golden light shed over the island, while sacred swans flew round encircling it seven times. This was in May, and for that reason his festival at Delos, the Delia, was held in that month. But Leto was compelled, through the pursuit of Hera, to abandon her children. They were entrusted to Themis, a name that signifies "justice," and indicates here the indisputable sense of right present with Apollo from his birth. By her he was fed on ambrosia and nectar, upon which he grew so strong, and that, too, so quickly, that within only a few hours after his birth he was a youth of dazzling appearance, and escaped his divine nurse, proclaiming that his destiny was to be a bowman, a player on the lyre, and to give truthful oracles to mankind.

To accomplish the end of his ambition he set out at once on a pilgrimage to search for a suitable place for an oracle, neither too public nor too retired. After searching through many districts of Greece he arrived at the quiet rocky valley of Delphi, which he recognized as the desired spot, on account of its peaceful position in the heart of Greece. Moreover there had been an oracle of Themis there from a remote early time, and she was willing to hand over her duties to the young god. A terrible dragon, however, called Python, stood in the way, refused entrance, and tried to repel him; but in vain, for the young god, confident in the unerring aim of his arrows, attacked the monster, and slew it after a short combat. In this way he acquired his world-famed oracle, and from his victory over the dragon obtained the title of Pythios.

From that time forward, with one exception, Apollo remained in undisputed possession of the sacred tripod and oracle at Delphi, and that was when he had to take up their defense against Hercules, who, because the acting priestess did not prophesy as he wished, offered her violence and carried off the tripod. Apollo hastened to the aid of his priestess, and Zeus had to settle the quarrel between his two sons, who thereafter lived in the closest friendship.

He like his brothers and sisters had his hands full with family feuding and quarrels and was constantly trying to dethrone his father. Amongst the other incidents of his life, it is related that Apollo once incurred the severe displeasure of Zeus, and was driven for a time out of Olympos, through having shot at some of the Cyclops in revenge for Zeus having struck Asklepios (Esculapius), a son of Apollo, with a thunderbolt. During his exile on earth he acted as a herdsman to his friend Admetos, the king of

Pheras, in Thessaly, and again in the same capacity to Laomedon, prince of Troy. In vexation at his banishment he joined with Poseidon in an attempt to dethrone Zeus. But the scheme failed, and both deities were in consequence sentenced to assist in building the walls of Troy. Laomedon refused to give them the payment agreed on for the service, and Apollo avenged himself by sending a dreadful pestilence that depopulated the town and neighborhood of Troy.

Apollo was a disagreeable character who was not afraid to inflict supernatural punishment on those who did not repeat his words back to him as divine wisdom. He was particularly sensitive when the topic of argument came to that of musical instruments. During the time of his servitude he had also a quarrel with Pan, who insisted that the flute was a better instrument than the lyre. The decision, which was left to Midas, a king of Lydia, was given in favour of Pan, for which Apollo punished Midas by causing his ears to grow long like those of a donkey. Marsyas, too, had boasted that he could surpass Apollo in the art of playing on the flute, and for this had to suffer the cruel punishment of being flayed alive.

He himself became a deadbeat dad, and as a result his relations with his children led to many unpleasant moments. Of the sons of Apollo the most famous is Phaethon, of whom it is said that he once had a dispute about his origin with Epaphos, a son of Zeus and Io, and in consequence begged Apollo, if he really was his father, to prove himself such by granting one request; upon which Apollo called the river Styx to witness that he would not refuse to grant it. The request was, that he, Phaethon, should be permitted for one day to drive the chariot of the sun. Apollo, astonished at the boldness of the request, and alarmed at the danger that threatened his son in such an undertaking, endeavored to move him from his determination. But Phaethon only clung to the bargain all the more firmly, and Apollo, finding himself bound by his oath, instructed his son how to drive and manage the horses, and handed over to him the task for one day. The youth, however, through being unused to the work, and unacquainted with the right way, soon became confused, and lost his strength and his senses.

Absentee fatherhood was never a good thing, but in the case of Apollo's relationship to his son, it almost led to the incineration of the earth. The spirited horses wheeled out of the right course, and brought the chariot of the sun so near to the earth that in some places the latter took fire, fountains were dried up, rivers began to boil, and part of the human race became black in colour. Zeus, alarmed at the unexpected danger in which both heaven and earth were thus placed, slew Phaethon with a stroke of lightning, and cast him from the chariot of the sun down into the river Eridanos. The three sisters of Phaethon, Heliades, as they were called — that is, daughters of Apollo, Phaethusa, Jegle, and Lampetia, wept for him a long time, and finally became transformed into larch trees, that overhang the river's banks, the tears that continually flowed from them being changed by the sun into amber (elektron). Phaethon's friend Kyknos mourned his loss deeply, and was transformed into a swan, while Apollo was so grieved at his son's death that only the entreaties of the gods could prevail on him to resume the reins of the chariot of the sun.

Dionysus

The belief in the existence and powers of Dionysus appears to have been borrowed by the Greeks in its primitive form from oriental mythology, to have been developed by them, and in later times communicated to the Romans. His original signification was that of a divine being whose power might be noticed operating in the sap of vegetation; and, accordingly, spring was a season of gladness and joy for him, and winter a season of sorrow. From this sprung his double character of god of the vintage and its accompaniments, and god of the ecstatic and mystic ceremonies in which his sufferings during winter were deplored. As time went on he came to be viewed chiefly as the source of the happiness and mirth which arise from the enjoyment of the noble fruit of the vine; while afterwards, from the fact that his festivals in spring and summer, with their gaiety and mirth, gave occasion to the first attempts at dramatic performances, he added the function of god of the theatre to that of god of the vine. In short, he could be capable of some appalling behavior, but nobody could come to dislike him.

His birth, as we have seen happen many times already, was due to Zeus's philandering. He was born, it was commonly believed, at Thebes, and was a son of Zeus and Semele, a daughter of Kadmos, the founder of that town, a son of Agenor, and grandson of Poseidon. Of his birth poets relate how Hera, indignant at this rival in her husband's affections, determined to get rid of her; and to this end, assuming a disguise, went to Thebes, and presented herself to Semele; how she succeeded in winning her confidence, and thereupon took occasion to propose that she should ask Zeus to visit her for once in all the plenitude of his majesty as god of thunder, how Zeus, who, without waiting to listen, had hastily sworn "by the black waters of the Styx," to grant whatever she should ask, was vexed when he heard the foolish request, from granting which no power could absolve him; how one day he appeared before the luckless Semele with a display of thunder and lightning which caused her death. So far the

desire of vengeance on the part of Hera was satisfied. But Semele, at the moment of her death, gave birth to a male child, whose life Zeus fortunately restored. That was the child Dionysus. To prevent its suffering at the hands of Hera, Hermes, the messenger of the gods, was secretly despatched with the infant to a place called Nysa, where were certain nymphs, to whom, along with Silenos, the charge of bringing up the child was entrusted. His title of Dithyrambos, it is said, means " twice born," and refers to the incident of his life being restored by Zeus. In after times it was applied to a species of song in honor of the god of wine, of which Arion of Methymna was the reputed originator.

He became known for teaching proper wine cultivation. He was also a partier that could quickly turn vicious if somebody got on his bad side. The childhood of Dionysos was spent in innocence and happiness among the nymphs, satyrs, sileni, herdsmen, and vinetenders of Nysa. But when he arrived at manhood he set out on a journey through all known countries, even into the remotest parts of India, instructing the people, as he proceeded, how to tend the vine, and how to practice many other arts of peace, besides teaching them the value of just and honorable dealings. He was praised everywhere as the greatest benefactor of mankind. At the same time, it is said, apparently with reference to the fierce and stubborn mood that in some cases follows copious indulgence in wine, that he met occasionally with great resistance on his journey, but always overcame it and punished those who opposed him most severely. As an instance of this, we will take Lykurgos, the king of Thrace, whom, for his resistance, Dionysos drove mad, and caused to fell his son, mistaking him for a vine-plant, and afterwards to kill himself in despair. Or, again, Pentheus, a king of Thebes, whom he caused to be torn to pieces by his own mother and her following of women, because he had dared to look on at their orgiastic rites.

Nobody threw a festival like Dionysus, and nowhere was the knowledge of how to utilize the vine appreciated more than in Attica, where the god had communicated it to Ikaros, whose first attempt to extend the benefit of it to others brought about his own death, an event which was deeply grieved for afterwards. In December a festival, with all manner of rustic enjoyments, was held in honor of Dionysos in the country round Athens. In January, a festival called Lenaea was held in his honour in the town, at which one of the principal features was a nocturnal and orgiastic procession of women. Then followed in February the Anthesteria, the first day of which was called ' cask-opening day,' and the second ' pouring day.' Lastly came the great festival of the year, the Great Dionysia, which was held in the town Gf Athens, and lasted from the ninth to the fifteenth of March, the religious part of the ceremony consisting of a procession in which an ancient wooden image of the god was carried through the streets from one sanctuary to another, accompanied by excited songs. The theatre of Dionysos was daily the scene of splendid dramatic performances, and the whole town was astir.

Hermes

Hermes was the first animal rights activist. He was a son of Zeus and Maia, a daughter of Atlas, and was regarded in the first instance as the special deity to whom was due the prolificness and welfare of the animal kingdom. This title, however, was soon supplanted by his title as the wealth, commerce, and closing a deal

– making him the Donald Trump of Mount Olympus. In consequence, however, of the fact that in early times the chief source of wealth consisted in herds of cattle, the prolificness of which was traced to him, it came to pass in time that he was considered generally to be the first cause of all wealth, come whence it might. But as civilization advanced, and it became known by experience that there was no means of acquiring wealth so rapidly as by trade, his province was extended to trade, and the protection of traders. Again, since the main condition of prosperity in trade was peace and undisturbed commerce by land and sea, he came to be viewed as guardian of commerce. And, further, assuming that all who took part in trade were qualified- to look after their own interests, shrewd and prudent, the function of protecting prudence, shrewdness, and even cunning, was assigned to him. In certain aspects of trade, if not in the best, it was reckoned a great point to talk over and cajole purchasers, and from his protection of this method of doing business, Hermes came to be god of "persuasive speech" or oratory. Finally, it being only a short step from this to cunning and roguery, we must not be surprised to find him described as protector of thieves and rascals, though no doubt this task was assigned him more in joke than in earnest.

He also worked as a divine carrier pigeon. His office of messenger and herald of the gods, in particular of Zeus, appears to have originated partly in the duty assigned to him of protecting commerce, the success of which depends largely on the messengers and envoys employed in it, and partly in other functions of his which would lead us too far to explain. As messenger and envoy of Zeus, Hermes conducts the interaction between heaven and earth, announcing the will of the gods to men, and from this office was further derived his character of a god of oracles. In the capacity of messenger or herald he had access even to the under-world, whither, under the title of Psychopompos, he guided the souls of the departed, crossing in Charon's bark, and placing them before the throne of the deities below. From the shadowy world of spirits to that of sleep and dreams is a short step for the imagination, and accordingly we find Hermes described as Oneiropompos, guide of dreams.

In proportion to the variety of the tasks which he had to perform was the variety of mythical stories about his actions and life, some of them taking us back to the very day of his birth. For it was not an uncommon practice in the early myth-making age to ascribe to the infancy of a god some instance of the peculiar qualities by which he was afterwards distinguished. So it happened with Hermes.

He was shrewd literally from the first day of his life. Born, as it was believed, during the darkness of night, in an unfrequented, lonesome cave on Mount Kyllene, he was only a day old when a remarkable example of his cunning and knavery occurred. Slipping out of the couch in the cave where he was left asleep as was supposed, the night being dark and cloudy, he found a herd of cattle belonging to his brother

Apollo and stole a number of them. When the morning came Apollo searched in vain for the missing cattle; for the infant god had cleverly succeeded in obliterating all traces of them by fastening bunches of broom to their hoofs, and in this condition driving them backwards into a cave at Pylos, so as to produce the impression that they had left instead of entered the cave. After this adventure he slunk back to his couch, and feigned to be asleep. He had, however, been observed by a rustic named Battos, who informed against him, whereupon Apollo, angry at such a daring piece of robbery, dragged him out of his couch, and took him off to the throne of Zeus to be punished and made an example of.

But Hermes was irrepressible and capable of escaping any punishment. He took up a lyre which he had made the day before out of the shell of a tortoise, and proceeded to play on it, to the amusement and delight of both Zeus and Apollo, and further ingratiated himself with his brother by giving him the lyre, inventing for his own use a shepherd's pipe. The cattle of the sun god were the clouds, and Hermes was a god who presided over the fertility of nature. The signification of the story of his stealing some of these cattle on a dark night would therefore seem to be simply that of clouds discharging fertilizing showers by night.

The two brothers having thus made their peace, continued from that time forward on the best of terms, Apollo attesting his good disposition towards Hermes by giving him in return for the lyre a present of a golden divining-rod, and also the power of prophecy. This condition, however, was attached to the gift, that he was not to communicate his revelations of the future by words as did Apollo, but by signs and occurrences. That is to say, that persons revolving some undertaking in their mind were to be guided by certain unexpected sights, accidents, or incidents, and were to recognize in them the favor or displeasure of the gods with reference to the enterprise in question, — a method of proceeding common enough in modern superstition. A simpler way to say this is that Hermes became the patron of gambling. These signs and incidents were believed to be sent by Hermes, whose counsel in other cases of doubt, as to whether to do or not do a thing, was sought for by recourse to dice, the belief being that a high throw signified his approval, and a low throw the reverse.

He was also something of a kleptomaniac. The cunning and adroitness, the same good humor and ready answer which he gave proof of in the first days of his infancy, were often afterwards and with like success displayed by him — as, for example, when he stole the scepter of Zeus, Aphrodite's girdle, Poseidon's trident, the sword of Ares, the tongs of Hephaestos, or Apollo's bow and arrows, in each case managing to make up matters, and smooth away the indignation of his victims. But the most celebrated instance in which his brilliant talents were fully displayed was the affair of Argos with the hundred eyes, whom Hera had appointed to watch over Io, one of the favorites of Zeus, whom the latter, that she might escape the vengeance of the jealous Hera, had transformed into a cow, a trick which the goddess had perceived.

Well, Hermes being commanded by Zeus to release Io from the surveillance of Argos, and in doing so to use no force, found the task no easy matter, seeing that the watchman had a hundred eyes, of which, when in his deepest sleep, only fifty were closed. Hermes succeeded, however, and in this fashion. Presenting himself to Argos, he commenced to amuse him by telling all kinds of tales, and having by these means fairly gained the watchman's confidence, he next produced a shepherd's pipe, and played on it various tunes of such sweetness that they gradually lulled Argos into so deep a sleep that one by one all his hundred eyes closed. The moment the last eyelid drooped Hermes slew him, and at once released Io, and led her away. For this service he rose high in the estimation of Zeus, and from that time the name of "Argos-slayer," Argei-phontes, was the proudest title that he bore. As a memorial of Argos, Hera, it was said, set his eyes in the tail of her favorite bird, the peacock.

But these and such-like instances of his knavery and cunning do not by any means express the whole character of Hermes; for his skill was also directed frequently to purposes of useful invention. It was he, for example, who invented Apollo's lyre, as well as that one by which the Theban musician, Amphion, did such wonders; and it was he who taught Palamedes to express words in writing. And, besides, wherever danger that required skill and dexterity as much as courage presented itself, he was always present to assist. He acted as guide to heroes in their dangerous enterprises, and in that capacity frequently, as in the case of Hercules, was associated with Athena. To travelers who had lost their way he was a ready guide, and to exiles a constant and willing helper in strange lands and among ill-disposed people.

He was also something of a Dwight Eisenhower, in that he streamlined continental travel for the Greeks. A messenger himself, it became his office to aid human messengers and travelers, and to this end it was he who inspired the idea of erecting sign-posts at cross-roads with directions as to whither each road led. These sign-posts took the form of statues, if they may be so called, consisting of a pillar running narrower towards the foot, and surmounted by ahead of Hermes, and called Hermae. It was the duty of travelers on passing one of them to place a stone beside it, a custom which not only largely helped towards clearing the fields of stones, but also led to improvement in the roads themselves, and hence to increased facilities for commerce. If more than two roads crossed, a corresponding number of heads were placed on the pillar, one facing each way. Similar figures were also found outside houses in Athens for the purpose of cheering parting travelers.

Chapter 2: Lower Gods and their Low-Down Behavior

In the last chapter we looked at the twelve gods that dominate the Greek pantheon and their less-than-flattering descriptions. While they clearly dominated the religious landscape in the polytheistic belief system and had the power to significantly influence events on earth, whether for good or bad, Greek mythology was littered with thousands of other smaller level gods. The Mediterranean world did not have a well-structured religious system, unlike Catholicism or Mormonism, nor did it have an official list of gods. Therefore any village could have a god unique to itself that they could worship as much as it liked, even to the exclusion of Zeus or Artemis. Villages and localities treated its gods the way that towns and cities in Germany treat their locally-produced beers – as a beloved part of its character whose faults they often look over. As a result, inferior deities in mythology could be just as strange as their more powerful cohabitants on Mount Olympus, even if they did not have as much power. We shall now proceed now to the inferior order, such as occupied subordinate positions in the system to gods, but were nevertheless worshipped independently, it not so universally as the others.

Pan

The first god we shall consider is Pan, the namesake of the pan flute and enormously proud of his musical talent. He was looked upon by the pastoral inhabitants of Greece, particularly in Arcadia, as the god who watched over the pasture fields, herdsmen, and herds. Woods and plains, hunting and fishing, were under his immediate care and patronage, and on this account he was differently described as a son now of Zeus, now of Hermes, his mother being in each case a nymph. As god of green fields he was associated with the worship of Dionysos, and as mountain god with that of Kybele. He was fond of sportive dances and playing on the shepherd's pipe, which afterwards took its name of Pan's pipe from him, the story being that he was the inventor of it. It seems that a coy nymph named Syrinx, whom he loved and followed, was transformed into a reed, that Pan cut it and fashioned it into a pipe (Syrinx) and was enormously skillful. He was so confident in the sweet notes when skilfully played, that he once ventured to challenge Apollo to a competition, a competition that would have played out like an ancient equivalent of "The Devil Went Down to Georgia."

The judge selected was Midas, who awarded the prize to Pan, and was, in consequence punished by Apollo. Ever the sore loser, he made his ears grow like those of an ass. As god of herdsmen and country people, Pan journeyed through woods and across plains, changing from place to place like the nomadic or pastoral people of early times, with no fixed dwelling, resting in shady grottoes, by cool streams, and playing on his pipe. Hills, caves, oaks, and tortoises were sacred to him. The feeling of solitude and lonesomeness which weighs upon travelers in wild mountain scenes, when the weather is stormy, and no sound of human voices is to be heard, was ascribed to the presence of Pan, as a spirit of the mountains. And thus anxiety or alarm, arising from no visible or intelligible cause, came to be called " Panic fear," that is, such fear as is produced by the agitating presence of Pan.

Like other famous musicians, he managed to attract a large entourage. His common companions were Nymphs and Oreads, who danced to the strains of his pipe. Unfortunately, also like other famous musicians, he could be violent to those around him; they were not infrequently pursued by him with violence. It is said that he rendered important service to the gods during the war with the Titans, by the invention of a kind of trumpet made from a seashell, with which he raised such a din that the Titans took fright, and retreated in the belief that some great monster was approaching against them. Another story is, that Dionysos being once seriously attacked by a hostile and very numerous body of men on his way to India, was freed from them by a sudden terrible shout raised by Pan, which instantly caused them to retreat in great alarm. Both stories appear to have been invented to give a foundation for the expression "Panic fear."

Pan, also called Hylaeos or forest god, was

usually represented as a bearded man with a large hooked nose, with the ears and horns and legs of a goat, his body covered with hair, with shepherd's pipe (syrinx) of seven reeds, or a shepherd's crook in his hand. From Greece his worship was transplanted among the Romans, by whom he was styled Inuus, because he taught them to breed cattle, and Lupercus, because he taught them to employ dogs for the purpose of protecting the herds against wolves. The other forest deities, who were represented like Pan with goat's legs, were sometimes called Paniski.

Okeanos, Tethys, and Proteus

The next trio of gods represented elements of the sea and earth. As the Greeks typically worked as mariners or in the agricultural sector they were aware of the fickle nature of the environment. As a result they attributed this to the short-tempered, fickle nature of gods and Titans associated with these elements. Okeanos, a son of Uranos and Gaea, was god of the sea, and, like Nereus, was looked upon as the father of a large family of marine deities who went by the general name of Okeanides. He was figured like Nereus, but with the addition of a bull's horn, or two short horns, a scepter in his hand to indicate his power, riding on a monster of the deep, or sitting with his wife, Tethys, by his side in a car drawn by creatures of the sea. He is said to have been the most upright of his brother Titans, and to have had no share in the conspiracy against Uranos. For this reason he retained his office, while the other Titans were consigned to Tartaros. It was under the care of Okeanos and his wife that Hera grew up, and to them she turned for safety during the war with the Titans.

Being god of the sea meant having more offspring than a polygamist oil sheik. So quickly had his offspring spread among the rivers, streams, and fountains of the earth, that the sons alone were reckoned as three thousand in number. He was also identified with the great stream, Okeanos, which was supposed to flow in a circle round the earth, and to be the source of all rivers and running waters. His daughters, the Okeanides, were, like all marine deities, represented with crowns of sea-weeds, strings of corals, holding shells, and riding on dolphins, a depiction that was the forerunner of mermaids. Painters rendered them as half human and half fish in shape; but poets described them as beings of purely human form, giving their number very differently.

Proteus was a son of Okeanos and Tethys, whose proper dwelling-place was the depths of the sea, which he only left for the purpose of taking the sea calves of Poseidon to graze on the coasts and islands of the Mediterranean. Being an aged man, he was looked on as possessed of prophetic power and the secrets of witchcraft, though he would not be persuaded to exercise the former except by deceit or under threat of violence. Even then he made every effort to evade his questioners, changing himself into a great variety of shapes, such as those of a lion, panther, swine, or serpent, and, as a last resource, into the form of fire or water. This faculty of transformation, which both Proteus and Thetis possessed, corresponds with the great changeability in the appearance of the sea.

Leukothea was regarded by sailors and those who travelled on the sea as their special and friendly goddess, a character that she displayed in her timely assistance of Odysseus in his dangerous voyage. She is said to have been a daughter of Kadmos, the great-grandson of Poseidon. Originally the wife of Athamas, in which capacity she bore the name of Ino, she had incurred the wrath of Hera, because she had suckled the infant Bakchos, a son of her sister Semele and of Zeus, and for this was pursued by her raving husband, and thrown, along with her youngest son, Melikertes, into the sea, from which both mother and child were saved by a dolphin or by Nereides. As we can see from this episode, breastfeeding was a sensitive issue in the ancient world. From that time she took her place as a marine deity, and, under the name of Leukothea, was known as the protector of all travelers by sea, while her son came to be worshipped as god of harbors, under the name of Palaemon. Her worship, especially at Corinth, the oldest maritime town of importance in Greece, and in the islands of Rhodes, Tenedos, and Crete, as well as in the coast towns generally, was traced back to a high antiquity.

The Sirens

If you happen to be drinking from a Starbucks cup at the moment, take a look at the green figure that adorns its front. That is a picture of the Siren – the mythological figure that would lure in passersby with their seductive nature only to bring them to their ruin – much like Starbucks coffee itself. According to one version of the myth, were daughters of the river-god Acheloos (hence their other name, Acheloi'des) and a Muse. According to another version, they were daughters of Phorkys. In either case they had been nymphs and playmates of Persephone, and for not protecting her when she was carried off by Pluto were transformed by Demeter into beings half woman and half bird at first, and latterly with the lower part of the body in the shape of a fish, so that they had some resemblance to marine deities such as the Tritons.

In the Homeric poems their number is not specified. In later times the names of three of them are commonly given: Parthenope, Ligeia, and Leukosia. It is said that once, during the time when the greater part of their body was that of a bird, they challenged the Muses to a competition in singing, but failed, and were punished by having the principal feathers of their wings plucked by the Muses, who decked themselves with them. As we see with this episode and the case of Pan, the gods took their musical competitions very seriously.

The common belief was that the Sirens inhabited the cliffs of the islands lying between Sicily and Italy, and that the sweetness of their voices bewitched passing mariners, compelling them to land only to meet their death. Skeletons lay thickly strewn around their dwelling; for they had obtained the right to exercise this cruel power of theirs on men so long as no crew succeeded in defying their charms. This the Argonauts, of whom more will be said hereafter, were the first to accomplish, by keeping their attention fixed on the sweet music of their companion, Orpheus. The next who passed safely was Odysseus. He had taken the precaution, on approaching, to stop the ears of his crew, so that they might be deaf to the bewitching music, and to have himself firmly bound to the mast, so that, while hearing the music, he would not be able to follow its allurements. In this way the power of the Sirens came to an end, and in despair they cast themselves into the sea, and were changed into cliffs.

This transformation helps to explain the signification of the myth of the Sirens, who were probably personifications of hidden banks and shallows, where the sea is smooth and inviting to the sailor, but proves in the end the destruction of his ship. The alluring music ascribed to them may either refer to the soft melodious murmur of waves, or be simply a figurative expression for allurement.

Nymphs

Due to their "gregarious" nature, the nymphs are the namesake for the psychological disorder of nymphomania. The restless and fertile imagination of the ancients peopled with beings of a higher order than themselves every mountain, valley, plain, and forest, every thicket, bush, and tree, every fountain, stream, and lake. These beings, in whose existence both Greeks and Romans firmly believed, were called Nymphs, and resembled in many respects the mermaids and fairies of modern superstition.

Generally speaking, the Nymphs were a kind of middle beings between the gods and men, communicating with both, loved and respected by both; gifted with the power of making themselves visible or invisible at pleasure; able to do many things only permitted to be done by the gods; living, like the gods, on ambrosia; leading a cheerful happy life of long duration, and retaining strength and youthfulness to the last, but not destined to immortality, like the gods. In extraordinary cases they were summoned, it was believed, to the councils of the Olympian gods, but usually remained in their particular spheres, in secluded grottoes and peaceful valleys, occupied in spinning, weaving, bathing, singing sweet songs, dancing, sporting, or accompanying deities who passed through their territories, hunting with Artemis (Diana), rushing about with Dionysos (Bacchus), making merry with Apollo or Hermes (Mercury), but always in a hostile attitude towards the wanton and excited Satyrs.

A famous example of this species was Echo, a mountain-nymph, and at the same time a servant of Hera, according to one account, but had to be kept at a distance on account of her talkativeness. In other accounts she is described as a beautiful nymph whom the forest-god Pan loved. Happening to meet the beautiful Narkissos, a son of the river-god Kephissos, she conceived a very tender passion for him, which he unfortunately did not return. Her overwhelming passion soon led to mental disorder. Echo grieved in consequence, and pined away day by day till at length her voice was all that was left of her. She then took to the mountains and woods that Pan frequented, and occupied herself in mimicking every vocal sound she heard.

Perhaps she was better off that her affections were not returned. Narkissos was a personification of the consequences of self-conceit in the matter of personal appearance, his vanity being such that he used to idle by the brinks of clear fountains, and gaze upon the reflection of his own face, till at last he languished in his unreturned love for it. Other stories affirm that he was punished for this conduct by the gods, by being changed into the flower that still bears his name.

The Wind Gods

All nature was anthropomorphized in Greek mythology, including the wind. The principal were Boreas, the north wind, Euros, the east wind, Notos, the south wind, and Zephyros, the west wind, were, as we have previously said, the offspring of Eos and Astraeos, the parentage of fierce destructive winds being assigned to Typhoin. According to another report, neither the origin nor the number of the deities of the winds was known, the prevalence in particular districts of winds blowing from this or that point between the four chief quarters, naturally giving rise to a set of personifications such as northwest wind, southwest wind, and others.

The character and appearance ascribed to each of these deities was, as usual in Greek mythology, such as was suggested by the phenomena of each wind as, for example, the strength and fury of the north wind, or the genial warmth of the southwest. Some were thought to be male, some female, and all winged. Euros, who brought warmth and rain from the east, was represented holding a vase inverted, as if pouring rain from it. Lips, who from the southeast wafted home the ships as they neared the harbor of Peireeus at Athens, held the ornament from a ship's stern in her hands. Zephyros, coming from the warm, mild west, was lightly clad, and carried a quantity of flowers in his scarf. Apeliotes, the southeast wind, carried fruits of many kinds, wore boots, and was not so lightly clad as the last mentioned. So they were represented on the " Tower of the Winds " at Athens.

The winds often kept to themselves, but they performed a vital military function in the Greco-Persian war. Though the winds were looked on as each under the control of a separate divine being, whose favor it was necessary to retain by sacrifice, no particular story or myth is told of any one of these persons excepting Boreas and Zephyros, the rival lovers of Chloris (Flora), Zephyros being the successful suitor. Boreas carried off, it was said, Oreithyia, the beautiful daughter of Kekrops, king of Attica; and remembering this, the Athenians in their distress, when the Persians advanced the first time against Greece, called upon him for aid, which he rendered by sending a terrible north wind, which overtook the Persian fleet near the promontory of Athos, scattered and largely destroyed it. From that time the Athenians had an altar to him, and offered sacrifice at it for their preservation.

Eos

Eos was the god of the morning and a connoisseur of young men. She was a daughter of the Titan pair, Theia and Hyperion; the latter, to judge from the meaning of his name, having been at one time god of the sun, "who travels high above earth." Helios and Selene, the deities of sun and moon, were her brother and sister, while she herself was a personification of the dawn of morning. A fresh wind was felt at her approach, the morning star still lingered in the sky, and ruddy beams "shot the orient through with gold" and because these beams appeared like outspread fingers, she was called "rosy-fingered Morn". The star and the winds of the morning, Zephyros, Boreas, Notos, and Euros, were her offspring by Astraeos, the god of starlight. The moon and the other stars vanished gradually as she advanced, but Helios followed her closely. To poets she seemed to lift the veil of night with rose-tinted fingers, and to rise in the east out of the ocean in a car with four white steeds, shedding light upon the earth. Others imagined her coming riding on the winged horse Pegasos, which Zeus had given her after Bellerophon's failure to ride on it up to Olympos.

She loved all fresh young life, and showed special favor to those persons whose active spirit led them abroad in the morning to hunt or to make war. When struck with the beauty of a youth she would carry him off, and obtain immortal life for him, as she did with Kleitos, Orion, Kephalos, and Tithonos. So it appeared to the Greeks, who recognized in the brief duration of the freshness and glow of morning a comparison with the early death of promising and beautiful youth, and from the comparison proceeded to construct a myth that should trace both to the same divine cause.

Her desire for youthful love left behind a tragicomic result. Tithonos became her husband, and she lived with him pleasantly beside the Okeanos so long as his youth and beauty lasted. Unfortunately, in obtaining immortality for him from Zeus, she had omitted to add to her request, "and eternal youth." When white hairs showed themselves on his head she was not the same to him as before, though still supplying him with ambrosia and fine raiment. But he became quite helpless at last, and, to avoid the sight of his decrepitude, she did the humane thing and shut him up in a chamber, where only his voice was heard like the chirp of a grasshopper, into which creature, it was said, he became transformed.

In the course of divine relationships, even remaining loyal to one's spouse could be dangerous. Of Kephalos it is said that from love to his wife, Prokris, he resolutely withstood the advances of Aura, the goddess of the morning wind, and that the latter in revenge stirred up discord between him and his wife. Another version of the story is, that Aura caused him to kill his wife by mistake when out on the chase. Prokris, it would seem, jealous of her husband's meetings with the goddess, had secreted herself in a thicket to watch them; but happening to stir Kephalos caught the noise, and suspecting it to be caused by some lurking animal, hurled his spear, and slew his wife.

Eros, or Amor: Psyche

With his quiver full of love arrows at his side, ready to inflict feelings of love on the willing and unwilling, this god was quite unpredictable. He also has a quite convoluted background and committed all sorts of mischief in iterations of his stories that we made before he became the chubby cherubim that we know today. Amor, or Cupid, as he was also called, was not, it should be noticed, a native Roman deity, but had been introduced from the mythology of the Greeks by poets, his name being a direct translation of the Greek Eros. It should further be observed that this translation presents an instance of the difference in character of these two ancient races; the word for "love" among the Greeks being feminine, while its Roman equivalent was masculine.

We must at the outset distinguish the double character of Eros; first, as we find him described taking part at the creation of the world out of Chaos, and secondly, as a mere god of love, a son of Aphrodite and Zeus, or Ares, as some said, or even of Uranos. In the former phase of his character he is represented as sorting the shapeless mass of the world, with its conflicting elements, into order and harmony, dispelling confusion, uniting hitherto jarring forces, and making productive what was barren before. In the latter phase he is the deity who sways the passions of the heart both of gods and men. In the one case he was conceived as having existed before the other gods, as being the god of that love which operates in nature ; and in the other case as the youngest born of them all, the god of that love which holds the hearts of men in tyranny. It seems to have been as a combination of both characters that Pheidias represented him at the birth of Aphrodite, receiving her as she rose out of the sea, in presence of the assembled deities of Olympos.

To the later age of Hellenistic and Roman poetry and art belongs the touching story of Psyche a personification, as she appears to have been, of a soul filled with the passion of love, and as such conceived under the form of a small winged maiden, or, at other times, as a butterfly which bore the same name. Psyche, the story runs, was a king's daughter, and most beautiful. The fame of her beauty awoke the jealousy of Aphrodite, who, to get rid of the rival, charged her son Cupid to visit the princess, and inspire her with love for some common man. Cupid obeyed so far as to pay the visit, but being himself struck with the maiden's beauty, carried her off to a fairy palace in a vale of paradise, where they spent happy hours together, with only this drawback, that she was not permitted to look upon her lover with her mortal eyes. Even this she would not have considered a drawback, had not her envious sisters stirred up her curiosity in the matter. Yielding to their temptation, she took one night a lamp, and stole into the chamber where the god lay asleep. Alarmed at the discovery she had made, she let a drop of hot oil fall upon his shoulder. He awoke, and charging her with disobedience to his express command, left her alone to her despair. She searched for him everywhere in vain, finding her way at last to the palace of Aphrodite, who, after subjecting her to menial service of various kinds, finally ordered her to go down to the lower world, and fetch a box of beauty's ointment from Persephone. This most painful task she accomplished; but on opening the box, sank overpowered by its odor. Cupid could resist no longer, ran to her help, and brought her back to life. The anger of Aphrodite was appeased, and the marriage of Cupid and Psyche was forthwith celebrated with great rejoicings, in presence of the higher gods, Psyche obtaining immortality.

The purpose of the story is obviously to

illustrate the three stages in the existence of a soul, its pre-existence in a blessed state, its existence on earth with its trials and anguish, and its future state of happy immortality. It also shows that relationships with gods is never an easy business.

Hymen, or Hymeneus

The meaning of this god's name should not be too difficult for the reader to deduce. Hymen, or Hymeneus, was worshipped as the god of marriage both by the Greeks and the Romans. Like many gods he was quite good-looking, but unfortunately for him he was also quite androgynous. This led to one of the first myths that involved cases of cross-dressing. His origin is variously stated to have been now from Apollo and Kalliope, now from Dionysos and Aphrodite, while at other times he is said to have been by birth a mortal, and afterwards deified. Properly speaking, he is a personification of the marriage song. There are various accounts of his life and deification, and among them the following:

Young, and of a soft delicate beauty, so that he might be mistaken for a girl, Hymen loved a young Athenian maiden, whom, however, because of his poverty, he could not hope to obtain for his wife. To be near her, he once joined a troop of maidens, among whom she was engaged in celebrating a festival to Demeter at Eleusis. Suddenly a band of robbers appeared from a hiding-place, carried the maidens off to their ship, and set out with the intention of selling them as slaves in some distant country. But landing on the way on a dreary island, the robbers indulged so copiously in wine that they all fell into deep slumber. Hymen, seizing the opportunity, incited his fellow-captives to take the weapons from the robbers and slay them all, which they did. Thereupon he set off to Athens in the ship, and finding the people there in great distress, presented himself to the parents of the maiden he loved, and undertook to bring her back unharmed on condition of their giving her to him as his wife. He probably did not mention at this point that his successful escape was the result of how effectively he passed himself off as a female.

This was readily promised. Finding a crew, he at once set sail for the island, and speedily returned with all the maidens on board. For this he obtained the title of Thalassios, as well as the wife that had been promised him. So happy was his wedded life that at marriage ceremonies generally his name was on the lips of all the company, and he himself in course of time came to be looked on as a god, and the founder and protector of marriage rights. At bridal festivities a sacrifice was offered to him, festal songs were sung, and flowers and wreaths strewn. As a result, he is the namesake of a particular body part closely associated with marriage celebrations.

Asklepios

This half-god was an expert physician so good

at his craft that he made the immortals jealous by helping humans cheat death. He was, according to the most common version of the myth, a son of Apollo and Koronis, a daughter of a Thessalian prince. At his birth his mother died, struck by the arrows of Artemis; but the father saved the child, and taking it to Mount Pelion, gave it in keeping to the famous physician, Chiron, who carefully instructed the boy from early youth onwards in the mysteries of the healing art, training him at the same time to expertness in the chase. In the former the pupil soon excelled the master, curing the most malignant diseases, and working real miracles with his art. There was but one whom his success could injure, and that was Pluto, the monarch of the lower world, who urged his complaint before Zeus. The latter, astonished at the boldness of a mortal in thus defying the decrees of fate, felled the great doctor with a thunderbolt, to the indignation of Apollo, who was only silenced by banishment from Olympos for some time. Hell hath no fury like a god scorned.

His story, though, has a happy ending, as he became the patron saint of the healing arts. After his death Asklepios was looked upon as a god in Greece; festivals called Asklepia were held in his honor, and temples were erected to him, of which the most celebrated was that at Epidauros, in the Peloponnesos. Thither even the Romans sent ten deputies once, to inquire the will of the oracle with regard to a pestilence that was raging in Rome. The deputies had hardly entered the temple, when from behind the gold-and-ivory statue of the god a serpent appeared, the symbol of Asklepios, and followed them through the streets of the town, on to the harbor, and into their ship. They received it joyfully as a happy portent, and set out homewards. On reaching Italy the serpent left the ship, and proceeded to a temple of Sculapius, in the town of Antium, but afterwards returned to the ship, and did not leave it again until, on going up the Tiber, it stopped at an island. Thereupon the pestilence ceased, and a temple was erected on the island to Esculapius, to commemorate the event. Thither patients were conveyed and cured — a short statement of the symptoms of each case, and the remedy employed, being inscribed on tablets, which were hung up in the temple, and were found to be a great boon to posterity.

The Harpys, Gorgons, and Other Unpleasant Characters

If one is called a harpy it is never meant kindly – the accuser declares that his recipient loves to torture their victims through cruel methods. The Harpys were creatures employed, according to the belief of the Greeks and Romans, by the higher gods to carry out the punishment of crime. They were three in number: Aello, Okypete, and Kelaeno, or Podarge; and were said to be daughters of the giant Thaumas and the Okeanid nymph Elektra. Their body was that of a bird, their head that of a woman and it would seem that they were originally goddesses of the storm, which carries everything along with it.

Their manner of punishing those whom they were sent to punish was to carry off all the food set before their victim, and devour it, or failing that, to render it uneatable. Being tantalized by having one's supper continually eaten before them and vomited up is never pleasant.

Their cruelty was eventually put to an end. put Among others who were punished in this way was Phineus, a king of Thrace, his crime having been cruelty towards his own son and contempt of the gods. For showing the Argonauts the way to Kolchis he was, however, freed from their persecution by Kalais and Zetes, the winged sons of Boreas, who, in gratitude, killed them. At other times, as the case of the daughters of Pandareos, they are described as carrying off their victims bodily from the earth; while, on the so-called Harpy tomb in the British Museum, they appear to be represented as demons of death carrying away the souls of deceased persons.

The Gorgons, by name Stheino, Euryale, and Medusa, were daughters of Phorkys and Keto. They, too, were victims of the gods' jealousy toward them. Two of them were believed to be immortal, while the third, Medusa, the youngest and most beautiful of them, was mortal. Medusa was not always the repulsive creature that we know of her as, but she became that way by engaging in a tryst in the temple of the prudish Athena. She loved Poseidon, and having met him once in the temple of Athena, to the desecration of that building, was punished by having her beautiful hair turned into snakes, thus making her appearance more ghastly than that of her sisters. Her face was terrible to behold, turning the spectator into stone. At last Perseus, finding her asleep, cut off her head with his curved sword, and presented it to Athena, who had assisted him in the enterprise, to be worn on her shield as a terror to her enemies.

The ancient poets describe the Gorgons generally as horrid, aged women, and frequently place them by the side of the Furies. In early times there was only one Gorgon, Medusa, instead of the three of later times. The winged horse, Pegasus, was the offspring of her and Poseidon.

The Graeme, daughters of Phorkys and Keto, were three in number: Deino, Pephredo, and Enyo. Their names unsubtly declare their character, as they meaning respectively "alarm," "dread," and "horror." The ladies managed to live up to these titles. Sisters and at the same time guardians of the Gorgons, they were conceived as misshapen hideous creatures, hoary and withered from their birth, with only one eye and one tooth for the common use of the three, and were supposed to inhabit a dark cavern near the entrance to Tartaros. If one wanted to see or eat they had to pass the appendage onto them so they could insert it into the proper cavity.

The belief in their existence seems to have been originally suggested by the grey fog or mist that lies upon the sea and is a frequent source of danger to the mariner. It is said that Perseus obtained from them the necessary information as to the dwelling of the Gorgons by seizing their solitary eye and tooth, and refusing to return them until they showed him the way. He knew the power of persuasion.

We end this chapter of the stories of the minor gods with a quick character study of Momus, who could be considered the ancient precursor to the Internet troll and the patron saint of such a person. He was deity whose delight and occupation was to jeer bitterly at the actions both of gods and men, sparing no one with his insinuations except Aphrodite, in whom he could find nothing to blame, and vexed himself to death in consequence. As an example of his behavior, it is said that he complained of the man that Prometheus had made, because there was not a window in his breast through which his thoughts might be seen. Like all critics, when he did not have anyone to bring down, his *raison d'etre* withered up, and he was no more.

Chapter 3: Heroes and the Gods who Exploited Them

Up until now we have looked at the divine beings in Greek mythology. We now turn our attention to heroes, those men and women who are similar to you and me, except with slightly superhuman characteristics. They also are involved in some of the best stories about the petty behavior of the gods. This is because in the stories of the gods interacting with each other, their immature impulses can never be completely played out. Since both sides of the conflict are immortal, they are merely jousting back-and-forth in a never-ending match. Heroes, on the other hand, are mortal and far more susceptible to fall under the whims of the gods, and for two reasons. The first is that they could easily arouse the jealousy of the gods. Heroes could easily win the hearts of men since they lived among them and suffered from the same weaknesses, thus making their bravery all the more apparent. As a result, men would forget to attend the temple of Zeus or Artemis and instead fawn over Hercules. The second reason is that they could greatly anger the gods. The strength and cunning of the heroes allowed them to frequently outsmart their divine opponents. The Argonauts and Odysseus often circumvented the gods' strategies of oppressing humans. The celestial creatures could stand a lot of things, but they could not afford to be mocked.

Heroes were a class of beings peculiar, it would seem, to the mythology of the Greeks. They were regarded partly as of divine origin, were represented as men possessed of godlike form, strength, and courage; were believed to have lived on earth in the remote dim ages of the nation's history; to have been occupied in their lifetime with thrilling adventures and extraordinary services in the cause of human civilization, and to have been after death in some cases translated to a life among the gods, and entitled to sacrifice and worship. They were described as having been the first sovereigns and legislators of the nation, and as the founders of all the kingly and noble families. Monsters that devastated particular localities were destroyed, the oppressed were set free, and everywhere order and peaceful institutions were established by them. They were, in short, the adventurous knights the history of whose deeds formed for the mass of the people the first chapter of the national history, and that in a manner worthy both of the civilization to which the nation had attained, and of the gods to whose influence the progress was due. The legends of their adventures furnished to poets and artists an inexhaustible treasure of striking figures, wonderful deeds, and strange events, while they formed at the same time a most powerful element in the national education.

Origin of the Heroes

The origin of the heroes is similar to that of

the gods, and for this reason they have quite similar and impetuous personalities. It has been suggested that the belief in these beings may have originated in later times, in an impulse to people the blank early pre-historic age with ideal figures of a sublime order of men, to whom the nation might look back with pride; or that it may have originated in a desire to dwell on the memory of distinguished persons who had actually existed, and in time, by so doing, to exaggerate their actions to a degree quite beyond human powers. But it is far more probable that, like the gods, the heroes had originally been divine personifications of certain elements of nature, and the legends of adventures ascribed to them merely a mythical form of describing the phenomena of these elements.

The idea, for example, of a long struggle and ultimate victory over grim enemies, which is so characteristic of these adventures, is the same idea that we find pervading the early myths, in which the powers of light are represented as struggling with, and finally overcoming, the powers of darkness. But while the gods always maintained their relationship to the elements of nature, of which they were divine personifications; marine deities for instance, dwelling in the depths of the sea, and celestial deities in the pure ether. The heroes, on the other hand, had ceased to be identified with any particular element, and though retaining the form, strength, and courage of gods, came in time to be regarded as men of a high order that had once inhabited Greece, but had passed away.

The legends, which, as we have said, had been intended to be the mythical descriptions of certain natural phenomena, were expanded so as to embrace the new variety of adventures which imagination with its wide scope now assigned to the heroes.

There appears to have been a time when the gods generally were in danger of being reduced in this manner to the condition of demigods or heroes, such events, for instance, as the war of Zeus with the Titans and Giants, the contests of Apollo with Tityos and Python, or of Dionysos with his enemies, being calculated, from their adventurous nature, to present their authors more in the light of heroes than of gods, and to form readily subjects for the epic poets, as indeed the contests of Dionysos did. This tendency was, however, arrested by the necessity of defining, for the purposes of worship, the provinces of the various deities. And this danger of being reduced made them quite petty in their dealings with heroes.

From that time the position of the gods was determined, while the heroes became less and less distinguishable from men, the legends concerning them assuming gradually more of a historical than of an ideal character. Traditions of early battles and victories that still lingered among the people, were made to circle round these imaginary heroes, who in time became the centers of all the earliest national recollections, the accredited founders of most of the elementary institutions of social life, and the guides of colonists.

Prometheus and the First Heroes

The origin of man is at its core a story of shoplifting. Among the various opinions in ancient times concerning the origin of mankind, the most generally accepted one appears to have been that in which it was asserted that man and all other forms of life had, like the gods, originally sprung from the common mother earth. In such a primitive condition of life, perhaps nothing was regarded as of greater importance, or more mysterious in its nature, than fire. Its beam dispelled the dread of darkness, and its warmth removed the chill of winter. The fire of the hearth was the centre of domestic life. At the forge, tools and weapons were fashioned. It was an emblem of the life of man, with its flash and sudden extinction on the one hand and the illumination of its prolonged blaze on the other. In storms it was seen descending from the sky, and in volcanic eruptions it was seen issuing from the earth. The source of it all was readily believed to be in the close keeping of the gods; and how mankind came to obtain the use of it was explained in the story of Prometheus.

Zeus, foreseeing the arrogance that would arise from the possession of so great a blessing, had from the first refused to transmit any portion of his sacred fire to men. Their deplorable condition, however, owing to the want of it, found a champion in the person of Prometheus (a son of the Titan Japetos), who had previously identified himself with the cause of humanity in a dispute that arose at Mekone as to the rightful share of the gods in all sacrifices offered to them. On that occasion an ox had been slaughtered as a sacrifice, and Prometheus, having wrapped up all the eatable parts in the skin of the animal as one portion, and having cleverly covered the bones and worthless parts with fat as the other portion, asked Zeus to select what he thought the better portion for the gods. Zeus, though perfectly aware of the deceit, chose the worthless parts, and more firmly than ever determined to withhold his fire from men.

Prometheus did not give up his plans for the divine heist. He resolved to obtain it for them, and succeeded in snatching some of it from the hearth of Zeus, or, as another version of the story has it, from the forge of Hephaestos in Lemnos. He was successful, but quickly suffered the wrath of Zeus. As a punishment, he was condemned to be chained alive to a rock in the remote Caucasus mountains, and to submit while every day a vulture came to gnaw away his liver, which daily grew afresh. For a long time he bore this suffering, and indeed would never have been released but for the secret which he possessed concerning the ultimate fate of the dominion of Zeus, who, for the purpose of learning the secret, permitted Hercules to shoot the vulture, to free Prometheus, and bring him back to Olympos.

Meantime the human race enjoyed the many benefits of fire, and continued to advance in civilization rapidly. The gods, naturally, wanted to cripple their condition. That their cup of happiness might be mixed with sorrow, Zeus ordered Hephsestos to fashion a woman of clay, of divine beauty, but possessed of all the weaknesses as well as charms of human nature. Athena instructed her in the industrial occupations of women, Aphrodite gave her grace of manners, and taught her the arts of a beauty, while Hermes qualified her for the part of flattering and soothing.

With the help of the Graces and Hors, Athena robed her with costly, beautiful robes, and decked her with flowers, so that, when all was done, Pandora, as they called her, might be irresistibly attractive to gods and men. Hermes conducted her to Epimetheus, who, though warned by his brother Prometheus to accept no gift from Zeus, yielded to the besetting weakness from which he obtained his name — that of being wise when it was too late. He received Pandora into his house, and made her his wife. She brought with her a vase, the lid of which was to remain closed. The curiosity of her husband, however, tempted him to open it, and suddenly there escaped from it troubles, weariness, and illnesses, from which mankind was never afterwards free. All that remained was Hope.

Argos

One of the stranger of the heroes in mythology was Argos, a multi-eyed monster who was also something of a cow whisperer. At the head of the Argive line of heroes stands Inachos, the river-god, a son of Okeanos, like all the other river-gods. With the nymph Melia for his wife, he became the father of Phoroneus and Io, of whom the former, according to Argive legends, was the first man upon the earth. Such services as Prometheus was elsewhere believed to have rendered to early civilization were there ascribed to Phoroneus. He was reputed to have founded the town of Argos, and to have established there the worship of Hera. With regard to Io, we have already related how she was loved by Zeus, and, to escape the jealousy of Hera, was transformed by him into a cow — how Hera, discovering the transformation, set a watch over Io, in the person of Argos, a giant with a hundred eyes, and how Hermes slew the watchman and released Io.

Another version of the story says that it was Hera who transformed Io into a cow, for the purpose of thwarting the love of Zeus for her. Argos had tethered her to an olive-tree in a grove sacred to Hera, between the towns of Mykenae and Argos, and was there keeping guard when Hermes arrived and slew him. Though set free, Io did not yet regain her human form, but was compelled to wander through distant lands in the form of a white horned cow, goaded by a vexatious insect sent by Hera. At last, on reaching Egypt, she obtained rest, was restored to her human form, and became the mother of Epaphos.

Io, the white horned cow, appears to have been a personification of the moon, like the Phoenician goddess Astarte, who was also represented in this form. Her wanderings were like the wanderings of the moon. Hera, who punished her, was the supreme goddess of the heavens. Argos, with his many eyes, reminds us of the stars. The slaying of Argos by Hermes was a favorite subject with ancient artists.

Epaphos became king of Egypt, and had a daughter called Libya (after the district of that name on the shore of the Mediterranean), who bore to Poseidon, the sea-god, two sons — Agenor and Belos. While the former became the head of a race that spread over Phoenicia, Cilicia, and on to Thebes in Greece, Belos remained in Egypt, succeeded to the throne, and marrying Anchirrhoe, a daughter of the Nile, had two sons, Egyptos and Danaos. The latter was appointed to rule over Arabia, the former over Libya. Egyptos had fifty sons, and Danaos the same number of daughters. A dispute arose between the two families, and Danaos yielding took ship with his daughters and sailed to Argos, pursued all the way by the sons of Egyptos. At Argos, the home of his race, he was kindly received by the reigning king, and protected against the pursuers.

The blood feud between the families continued and took a nasty, deceptive turn. The fifty daughters were ordered to perpetrate the most violent wedding night in history. The sons of Egyptos, it is said, having besieged Argos for some time, at length proposed to forget their difference with Danaos, and to marry his daughters. Without relenting in the least, he agreed to give his daughters to them in marriage, but to each daughter he presented a knife, and commanded them all to slay each her own husband on the marriage night. All obeyed his order except Hypermnestra, who, preferring to be regarded as of weak resolution than as a murderess, spared her husband, Lynkeus, and became the mother of the Argive line of kings. While Zeus approved the murderous deed of her forty-nine sisters, and sent Athena and Hermes to give them expiation, Hypermnestra was cast into a dungeon by her indignant father, her husband, Lynkeus, saving himself by flight. On being brought to trial she was however publicly acquitted; her husband returning to Argos, succeeded Danaos on the throne, and in after times was widely respected, among other things for having founded the great festival in honor of the Argive Hera. The prize of victory in the games that accompanied that festival was a shield, not a wreath, as was elsewhere usual; the tradition being that on the first occasion of these games Lynkeus presented his son Abas with the shield which had belonged to Danaos.

He was proud of his 49 daughters for carrying out his bloody political scheming and decided to repay his brood of black widows. Whether it was to obtain husbands for his daughters who had accomplished their own widowhood, or whether it was to decide among a multitude of suitors for their hands, Danaos held a kind of tournament, the victors in which were to be accepted as husbands. On the morning of the contest he arranged his daughters together on the course, and by noon each had been carried off by a victorious athlete, a scion of some noble house.

It was said that after death the Danaides, with the exception of Hypermnestra, were punished in Tartaros by having continually to carry water, and pour it in the vain endeavor of filling a broken cistern. It may be that this form of punishment was selected for them as the most suitable for women, who generally in Greece were the drawers of water. At the same time it was very suggestive of the dry parched soil of Argos, the streams of which were always dried up in summer.

From Abas, the son of Hypermnestra and Lynkeus, sprang the brothers Akrisios and Prcetos, famous for their hatred of each other from infancy onwards – a Cain and Abel story refashioned for Greek audiences. When they had grown up, Prcetos, finding himself constantly defeated in the fraternal encounters, fled to Lycia, and was there hospitably received by the king, Iobates, and the queen, Amphianax, whose daughter Sthenebcea, he married. With the assistance of a Lycian army he was reinstated in his rights of sovereignty over Argos and Corinth, fortifying himself in the citadel of Tiryns, while his brother Akrisios held out in that of Larisa. Of both citadels, the massive structures, now in ruins, still bear witness to the fierce assaults that must have been made upon them.

Prcetos had three daughters, whose exceeding beauty made them prizes that the noblest youth of the country sought to win. But they were haughty, despised the common usages of the times, scorned to take part in the worship of Dionysos, and made ridicule of the sanctity of

Hera's ancient image and shrine. For this they were punished by a form of insanity that drove them ever to wander restlessly among the woods and hills of Argos and Arcadia. It is further said that, being under the hallucination that they were cows, they lowed like kine as they wandered about. The father summoned Melampos, the prophet and priest, to work a cure upon his daughters, but on the prophet's stipulating a third of the kingdom as his reward, dismissed him again. The evil grew worse, for the other women of the country began to yield to the infatuation of abandoning their husbands and slaying their children. Melampos was recalled, and this time demanded an additional third of the kingdom for his brother, Bias. Prcetos agreed, and Melampos, collecting a body of active youths, pursued the three princesses over the mountains, and on to Sikyon, where the eldest of the three died, and the other two, after being purified, were given in marriage to Melampos and Bias respectively.

Returning to Akrisios, we find him troubled at the prospect of having no heir to his throne. To his question the oracle at Delphi replied that a daughter would be born to him, and that she would bear a son who would slay his grandfather, and rule in his stead. The daughter, Danae by name, was born, and to prevent the latter part of the oracle from being fulfilled, she was imprisoned in a subterranean chamber. But a shower of gold, sent by Zeus, penetrated to her, and she became the mother of an infant destined to fulfill the oracle and to become conspicuous among the ancient heroes. He was named Perseus, probably with reference to his being a son of Zeus, the great god of light, and to his having been born in darkness, in which respect, as in several others, he may be compared with Apollo, whose mother was Leto (darkness), while his father was Zeus. The shower of gold would thus signify a beam of golden light.

Akrisios, hearing the voice of the child, summoned his daughter to the altar of Zeus to give a solemn explanation of the circumstance. Disbelieving her story, he placed mother and child in a closed box, and committed them to the waves. After rocking about on the bosom of the sea, the box was at last carried towards the island of Seriphos, and was there caught in a net belonging to a fisherman named Diktys, who took the waifs to his house, and acted kindly by them. It was a very barren island, affording little but shelter to the families of fishermen that inhabited it. The chief or king of it was Polydektes, a brother of Diktys, just mentioned, and as notorious for the gaiety of his habits as was his brother for his simplicity. Struck with the beauty of Danae, and finding that her son Perseus stood in the way of the fulfillment of his desires, Polydektes became anxious to get rid of him, and gladly availed himself of the opportunity that presented itself when Perseus, not to be outdone in professions of loyalty, vowed that he would even fetch the head of the Gorgon Medusa for the king, should he wish it.

Perseus set forth sadly on his mission, but took courage when Hermes and Athena, who often lent their aid in heroic adventures, appeared to him, and led him to where the Graese lived three aged women, with only one eye and one tooth in common – the Gorgon sisters, whom we encountered in the last chapter. Perseus, seizing the indispensable eye and tooth, refused to give them back until they told him where to find the nymphs who had in keeping the helmet of Hades, the winged shoes, and the pouch necessary for his future movements. On arriving at where the nymphs lived, he obtained from them the objects in question, to which Hermes added the knife (harpe) with which he had cut off the head of Argos. Buckling on the winged shoes, he proceeded towards the Gorgons with the speed of a bird, the helmet of Hades making him invisible, but concealing nothing from his sight. It is further said that Athena instructed him how to approach Medusa without being petrified, as was usual, by her stare. To this end she gave him a shield of polished brass, on which, as in a mirror, he could see the reflection of the Gorgon, while he himself, unseen, advanced and cut off her head. The instant he had done this there sprang from the trunk of Medusa Pegasos, the winged horse, and Chrysaor, the father of Geryoneus. Perseus, placing the head quickly into the pouch which the nymphs had given him, hastened from the scene, pursued by the two sisters of Medusa for some distance.

Perseus would continue to form alliances with and antagonized the gods. Among his adventures on the way back to Seriphos were the turning of Atlas into stone because the giant refused to receive him hospitably, and the release of Andromeda, whom he found, on passing over Ethiopia, bound to a rock on the sea-share as a victim to a great sea-monster. She was a daughter of Kepheus and Kassiepeia, the king and queen of Ethiopia. The latter having vaunted herself equal in beauty to the Nereids, gave offense to them and to Poseidon also, who thereupon visited the country with a flood, and sent a dreadful monster from the sea to destroy both men and cattle. On appealing to the oracle of Amnion in Libya, Kepheus was told that the evil would not abate until he exposed his beautiful daughter, Andromeda, to the monster. Compelled by his subjects to yield, the luckless father took her to the shore, and chained her to a rock, in the position in which Perseus found her. Struck with her beauty, Perseus undertook to save her on condition that she should become his wife.

Kepheus agreed to this, and Perseus, after slaying the monster, unchained the maiden. She had, however, been engaged beforehand to Phineus, her father's brother, who, arriving with a strong body of soldiers, burst in upon the marriage feast. But the sight of the Gorgon's head turned them all to stone, and Perseus triumphantly carried off his bride.

Perseus continued to consolidate power by inflicting punishments on his enemies with the decapitated Gorgon head and making use of its mystical properties. Arriving at Seriphos, he found that his mother and Diktys were being persecuted by Polydektes, and obliged to seek protection at the altars of the gods. His course was to announce his arrival to the king, who at once assembled his nobles to witness how the young hero had kept his word. Perseus appeared in the assembly, and producing the Gorgon's head, turned the king and all his nobles instantly to stone. Not content with punishing in this manner the principal persecutors of his mother, Perseus is said to have turned the island itself into a great barren rock, and to have spared only the excellent Diktys and the fishing population attached to him. Even the frogs of the island became dumb, said an ancient proverb.

Having thus fulfilled his promise, and rescued his mother, Perseus handed over the winged shoes, the pouch, and the helmet that made him invisible, to Hermes, to be restored to the nymphs. The head of Medusa he gave to Athena, who ever after wore it on her shield. Accompanied by Danae and Andromeda, he set out for Argos to find his grandfather,

Akrisios, who, however, in the meantime having left Argos in consequence of an increasing dread lest the oracle should be fulfilled regarding his death, had established himself at Larisa in Thessaly. Thither Perseus proceeded, and found, on his arrival, the king, Teutamias, occupied with public games in honor of his deceased father. Perseus took part in the games, and by a fatality that justified the oracle, the disc which he threw fell upon the foot of Akrisios, and caused his death.

After burying his grandfather honorably at

Larisa, Perseus returned to Argos to his mother and wife, but instead of establishing himself there, exchanged Argos for Tiryns, which was then held by Megapenthes, a son of Prœtos, and soon after founded the ancient Mykense, with its massive walls, Perseus and Andromeda had two sons — Elektryon and Alkaeos. Alkmene, the mother of Hercules, was a daughter of the former, and her husband, Amphitryon, a son of the latter. It was also said that before leaving the court of her father, Kepheus, Andromeda had born a son, whom they called Perses, and left behind with his grandfather. From this Perses the Persian kings traced their lineage. The kings of Pontos and Cappadocia, claiming the same descent, introduced a figure of Perseus on their coins. In Tarsos and in Egypt also were traditions of ancient benefits derived from the Greek hero.

Crete

The island of Crete, which was a prison colony in Ottoman times, always attracted eccentric characters (its inhabitants are known as "Cretans" – an insult today that means "thick-headed"). The position of the island of Crete, its extent and fertility, appear to have attracted the early Phoenician traders to its shores. They founded the towns of Knosos and Gortys, and so developed the resources of the island as to give it a powerful ascendency over the other islands of the Archipelago, and extending to various districts of the mainland of Greece, including

Attica, as has just been said. They introduced the worship of Astarte and Moloch; and when, generations afterwards, the island had become completely Hellenised, through the successive immigrations of Achaeans and Dorians, there were still found current among the people legends that could only be explained in connection with the religion of the Phoenicians. Of this kind were the legends of Talos, Itanos, and the river Jardanos. The Greek immigrants settled in the towns that had been planted by the Phoenicians, adapting themselves to existing arrangements, it appears, and accepting the ancient traditions of the island as a basis for legends of a purely Greek construction.

These legends commence with Europa and her interactions with Zeus, who thought fit to win her attractions by transforming himself into a bull. Zeus saw and loved her while she was gathering spring buds near Sidon, where her father, Agenor (or Phoenix, as some said), was king. The god, transforming himself into a white bull, carried her off on his back over the sea towards the south coast of Crete, and landed with her in the district of Gortys and Phasstos, where Asterion was then the reigning king. Europa gave birth there to three sons, Minos, Rhadamanthys, and Sarpedon, who grew up under the care of Asterion, to whom Zeus had commended their mother. How familiar the people of the island must have been with the various phases of this legend, may be seen from the ancient coins of Gortys and Phgestos, with their representations, now of a bull alone, now of

Europa riding on him, and at other times of Europa seated among the branches of a plane tree.

The oldest traditions describe Minos as ruling the island with exemplary justice, extending its maritime power and its supremacy over the neighboring islands and countries. He established among his people a wise system of laws, which formed, it was believed, in after times, the basis of the legislation of Lykurgos. These laws, he said, were communicated to him by his father, Zeus, with whom he went every ninth year to hold communion in a sacred cave in the island. So high was his reputation for justice, that when he died, so people thought, he was appointed a judge in the lower world.

The wife of Minos was Pasiphae, a daughter of the sun- god Helios and Perseis. It is necessary to bear her parentage in mind for the sake of obtaining a right clue to the explanation of the legend concerning her. For, as a daughter of Helios and Perseis, she may well have been originally a goddess of the moon, and as such represented under the form of a white cow. Her name, Pasiphae, would be appropriate for such an office. She bore to Minos two daughters, Ariadne and Phaedra, of whom more will be told hereafter.

Problems started when he did not offer a proper animal sacrifice to an insecure god. Minos, it was said, on being chosen king of the island, proceeded to the sea-shore to offer, in presence of his people, a sacrifice to his father, Zeus, calling on the sea-god Poseidon to send up a victim for that purpose from the sea. Poseidon heard, and sent a shimmering white bull. In this act of compliance on the part of the sea-god, Minos perceived that his supremacy at sea was secured. Instead, however, of sacrificing the white bull, he placed it among his own herd that browsed near Gortys, a herd which is elsewhere said to have belonged to the sun-god. Poseidon, taking offense at the deceit, caused the bull to become wild, and at the same time inflamed the queen, Pasiphae, with an unnatural desire towards it. The bull broke from his stall, and was pursued by Pasiphae over hills and through woods, till finally the great artist Daedalus succeeded in holding him to the meadow, and in satisfying the desires of the queen, who afterwards gave birth to Minotaurs, a creature with the body and limbs of a man, and the head of a bull. Daedalus had now to employ his skill in making a vast labyrinth, with intricate winding passages, from which no one who entered could find his way out. Within it Minotauros was placed, and received as victims the persons sent to Minos periodically by tributary states. Such tribute, consisting of seven boys and seven girls of noble families, Minos had levied on Athens as a satisfaction for the murder of his son Androgeos by Egeus, the king of Attica. Every eight years the grievous levy was dispatched to Crete, till Theseus, the son of Egeus, put an end to it in a manner which we shall afterwards have occasion to relate.

Minos met his death at Agrigentum, in Sicily, whither he had pursued Daedalus, who had escaped from the labyrinth, into which he and his son Icarus had been thrown for making a figure of a cow for Pasiphae, so lifelike as to be mistaken by the herd. He had escaped by means of wax wings that he had made for himself and his son. The latter fell into the sea, and was drowned, while his father, reaching Sicily in safety, was received under the protection of King Kokalos, whose daughter killed Minos by pouring boiling water on his head while he was in a bath. Minos was buried there, and had a tomb erected in his memory.

Hercules

The most famous hero in Greek mythology obtained his renown by overcoming petty challenges issued forth by the gods – truly not a simple task. Though regarded sometimes as a god, and honored in the way appointed for immortals, it was chiefly as the hero of a long series of arduous labors, difficulties apparently insurmountable, and sufferings, that Hercules obtained the numerous honors paid to his memory throughout Greece. In the gymnasia, where the youth of every town were instructed in athletic exercises, the statue of Hercules was pointed to as a model of what a perfect athlete should be; while the tales of his wrestling with this or that giant were repeated as examples of fearlessness and extraordinary strength. Soldiers going to battle thought of his fatigues and ultimate triumphs. Laborers oppressed by toil relieved their sorrows by recalling the laborious incidents of his life. Even the Athenians valued the rugged, stubborn endurance of Hercules higher than the litheness and more perfect form of their own Theseus. So far, Hercules was looked upon merely as an example of extraordinary physical strength and patient toiling to the end; but in later times he came also to be held up as an ideal of virtue and duty, in which capacity a story invented by the sophist Prodikos concerning him, found great applause. That story was entitled "The Choice of Hercules," and represented him a being met at a crossway, while yet a youth, by two figures, Pleasure and Duty — the one promising him all possible enjoyments, the other a life of labor and trouble, if he would follow her. He chose to follow Duty.

According to the genealogy, Hercules was a son of Zeus and Alkmene, the wife of Amphitryon, a descendant of Perseus, and resident in Thebes. On the day on which he was to have been born, Hera, to whose persecution all the labors and sufferings of Hercules in after life were due, obtained from Zeus, in presence of the assembled gods, a vow that the boy to be born on that day should have power and dominion over all that dwelt about him. Hastening to Argos, she lent a helping hand to the wife of Sthenelos, and enabled her to give birth to Eurystheus, a weakly seven-months-old child. Meantime she had delayed the birth of Hercules, who, in consequence, became the subject of Eurystheus. With all this hostility on the part of Hera, it is curious to compare a scene that not infrequently occurs on ancient painted vases, representing Hera suckling the infant Hercules. The story was that Hermes, at the command of Zeus, had carried the newly-born child to Olympos, and put it to Hera's breast, without her knowing whose child it was. From this divine milk Hercules drew his godlike strength, the first promise of which was given soon after his birth, by his strangling the serpent sent by Hera to kill him.

His youth was spent under the instruction of the most celebrated heroes of the day, the wise Rhadamanthys teaching him to be wise and virtuous, and Linos the practice of music. Unluckily, Linos had to punish him for some neglect, and in doing so enraged the boy so much, that he turned and slew his master. For this Amphitryon carried his son away to the hills, and left him under the care of herdsmen, with whom, like Romulus, or Amphion and Zethos, he enjoyed a wild life of hunting and exposure to climate, his limbs growing to enormous size, and his eyes sparkling with unusual fire. At the age of eighteen he slew an enormous lion that infested Mount Kithgeron, destroying the flocks of his father, Amphitryon, and of Thespios, the king of Thespiae. Returning to Thebes from the lion-hunt, and wearing its skin hanging from his shoulders as a sign of his success, he met the heralds of the king of the Minyae, coming from Orchomenos to claim the annual tribute of a hundred cattle levied on Thebes. Hercules cut off the ears and noses of the heralds, bound their hands, and sent them home. A war followed, in which Amphitryon and his two sons, Hercules and Iphikles, did wonders on the part of Thebes, and were duly honored for the same. But the part taken by Hercules in that war was the last act of his own free will; for Hera, annoyed at the fast-rising fame of the young hero, persuaded Eurystheus to exercise the authority given him at his birth by Zeus, and to call on Hercules to enter his service. Hercules inquired at the Delphic oracle whether it was possible to escape the summons, but was told in reply that he must carry out successfully twelve tasks to be imposed on him by Eurystheus, and that, having done so, he would be reckoned among the number of immortals. With this answer in his mind, he presented himself to Eurystheus at Mykena, and commenced the serious labor of life.

The Twelve Labors of Hercules

Many believe that the labors of Hercules were intended to convey an illustration of the course and operations of the sun. His first labors are performed near home, the distance from which increases with each new labor that is imposed, till at last, after carrying off the golden apples of the Hesperides in the remote west, he descends to the lower world, and brings back with him the hated dog Cerberus. Whatever their astronomical significance, they clearly were not easy.

In later times the twelve labors were openly brought into connection with the twelve signs of the zodiac. It is, however, more likely that, originally, this number had no more signification than in the case of the twelve higher deities of Olympos. In Homer, though the labors are known, there is no mention of their number. In the Iliad (v. 395) Hercules is the hero whose unerring arrows wounded Hera and Hades. In the Odyssey (viii. 224) Hercules and Eurytos are described as the most celebrated marksmen of bygone times; and in early works of art, it is his character as a bowman that is principally represented. But after the time of Pisander and Stesichoros, a change is introduced. The club becomes his favorite weapon; and instead of a linen garment wrapped round his loins, he now appears either carrying the skin of the Nemean lion over his arm, or wearing it hanging down his back — the skin of its head fitting to his crown like a cap, and the fore-legs knotted under his chin.

Let us now look at Hercules's twelve labors, and the Sisyphean ordeals that the gods put him through.

1. The Nemean lion, the offspring of Typhon and Echidna, had been sent by Hera to devastate the neighborhood of Nemea, and had succeeded, to the horror of the natives. What made the matter worse, was that the plain of Nemea was sacred to Zeus. The lion was known to be invulnerable, proof even against the arrows of Hercules. It was therefore necessary to adopt novel means for its destruction. Hercules entered the cave where its lair was, closed the entrance behind him, and at once grappling the monster in his arms strangled it. The skin he tore off with his fingers, and, knowing it to be impenetrable,

resolved to wear it henceforth in his own defense – using it as something of an ancient version of Kevlar. To the legend as it thus stands was added, by the Alexandrian and Roman poets, the story of Molorchos, a native of the district, on whom Hercules called on his way to the cave, and who, when about to kill his only goat to make a feast for his guest, was told by the hero to desist and to wait his return. It was arranged that should he not return within thirty days Molorchos was to sacrifice to him as to a dead person. The thirty days had just elapsed when Hercules returned and found his friend in the act of preparing the sacrifice.

2. The Lernean hydra, also the offspring of Typhon and Echidna, and sent by Hera. Hercules killed it with his sword, being assisted in the enterprise by Iolaos and Athena. The hydra was a monster with nine heads, of which eight were mortal and the ninth invulnerable. It lived in the marshy ground beside the fountain of Amymone, and even the smell which spread from its poison was fatal to any one who passed near it. Hercules arrived at the spot in a chariot, attended by Iolaos, and succeeded in driving the hydra from its hole by firing his arrows in upon it. The fight began, and Hercules found that for every head of it which he cut two fresh heads started up, and to increase the difficulty a huge crab came and seized him by the heel. It was necessary to try another form of attack. Hercules ordered Iolaos to set the neighboring wood on fire and to fetch him a brand from it; with the brand so obtained he proceeded, the moment he had cut off a head,

to burn it up, and in this way destroying them one by one, he at last came to the invulnerable head, cut it off also, and buried it under a huge rock. He dipped his arrows in the poison of the hydra. When his success was reported to Eurystheus, the latter refused to reckon it as one of the labors, on the ground that Iolaos had rendered assistance.

3. The Erymanthian boar, like the Keryneian Stag and the Stymphalian Birds, carries us to a mountainous and wild rustic scene. Its haunt was on Mount Erymanthos, in the north of Arcadia. The orders of Eurystheus were that the boar should be brought back alive to Mykense; but at the sight of Hercules returning with it alive on his shoulders, fear took possession of the king, and he hid himself in a large bronze vessel, into which Hercules, as frequently represented on ancient vases, proceeded to put the boar, as the safest possible place. The consternation of Eurystheus may be imagined. In connection with the capture of the boar is told the story of a visit which Hercules paid on his way to the Centaur, Pholos, who lived in a cave on Mount Pholoe. The hero was hungry, and Pholos gave him to eat. He was also thirsty, and required some wine. Now Pholos had at hand a large vase full of choice wine, but it was the common property of the Centaurs who lived in other parts of the mountain. On the other hand the wine had been a present from Dionysos, and had been accompanied with the command that it should not be opened till his good friend Hercules arrived. Pholos accordingly had no hesitation in

tapping the vase, and both drank deeply from it. The strong aroma of the wine, however, reached the nostrils of the other Centaurs, who now flocked towards the cave of Pholos in wild confusion, armed with pine branches, rocks, axes, and torches, and fell upon Hercules. A violent fight ensued, in which Hercules, besides with superior numbers, had also to contend with the disadvantage of a flood of water sent by the clouds, who were the mothers of the Centaurs. Ultimately he succeeded in wounding many, and dispersing the others into the woods, the only melancholy part of the issue being that his friend Pholos lost his life, under circumstances which remind us of the death of that other kindly Centaur, Chiron, who lived on Mount Pelion, and brought up Achilles. Pholos was stooping over a Centaur who had fallen by an arrow from Hercules, and after drawing out the arrow, was wondering how so small a thing could produce such an effect, when it fell from his hands, and striking severely on his foot, its poison entered his body and he died.

4. The Keryneian stag, an animal of wonderful fleetness, with antlers of gold and hoofs of brass, was sacred to Artemis, to whom it had been dedicated by Taygete, one of the Pleiads. The task imposed on Hercules was to capture and bring it back alive. The chase lasted for a whole year, Hercules pursuing it over hills and plains, ravines and meadows, on to the Hyperborean region, and thence back to where it had started among the Arcadian hills. It sought shelter in the sanctuary of Artemis, but being

dislodged was overtaken by Hercules at the banks of the river Ladon. He would have slain it had not Apollo and Artemis appeared on the scene. The stag running a whole year on to the regions of the Hyperboreans, and thence returning to where it had set out, appears to be a mythical illustration of the course of the moon, and may be compared with the much simpler story of the huntress Arge, the "shimmering being" who pursued a stag, crying out, "I will catch you should your speed equal that of Helios"; for which boast the angry god transformed her into a deer.

5 . The Stymphalian birds. The vale of Stymphalos, lying among the mountains in such a way as to be constantly exposed to the floods and storms of winter, was described in a mythical form as being subject to the ravages of a numberless flock of birds, which, with their iron talons and feathers sharp as arrows, delighted in human flesh. From the description of the figures of some of them, which were preserved in the sanctuary of Artemis, it appears that they resembled in form the Harpys, and like them, too, they were, there is every reason to believe, symbols of the cold, destructive storms of winter. To get rid of them, Hercules first raised an alarm by ringing a large bell; and when the birds came out from the thick wood where their nests were, many were shot down by his arrows, and the rest flew away in fright. They flew, as it appears from the story of the Argonauts, to an island, sacred to Ares, in the inhospitable Black Sea, where the Argonauts suffered severely from the heavy falls

of their sharp biting feathers, and only obtained relief by again frightening them by raising a great din. As the birds flew over the sea their feathers fell like a thick snowstorm, the flakes of which, it should be remembered, are frequently in the legends of other peoples compared with feathers. Hercules, as a hero representing the influence of the sun, was very properly called in by the myth-makers to destroy beings of this kind, more especially as in the neighboring district of Pheneos he had long been regarded as a beneficent hero. The statement of his having alarmed the birds by ringing a bell may have been suggested by a common practice of raising birds from their nests. At the same time it may also refer to a custom that is known at any rate in more recent times — that of ringing bells during severe storms, from a belief that such a proceeding availed against all evil spirits of the air.

6. The Augeian stables. This task was far less glamorous than the previous five and showed how functionalistic mythology could be. Augeias, the rich prince of Elis, and his daughter Agamede, the sorceress who knew the potency of all the herbs in the world, were known to the author of the Iliad (xi. 701, 739). His seat was at Ephyro, a name that occurs in connection with the worship of the heavenly powers, while Augeias itself means " a being of streaming light." Another feature of the story, which confirms the opinion that Augeias in some way was intended to illustrate the phenomena of the sun's light, is his possession of herds of lambs

and cattle, fabulous in numbers as are the fleecy clouds, and including twelve bulls, white as swans, and sacred to Helios — one of them being called Phsethon, and described as glittering like a star. The court of Augeias was by the banks of the river Menios, and the task assigned to Hercules was to clear out his endless line of stalls alone and in one day. To accomplish this, the hero made an opening through the wall at a part where the river approached it. The stream, rushing in at the opening, swept with it, as it flowed along the stables, their accumulated dung. Augeias had promised to reward Hercules with a tenth of his herds; but declined to fulfill his agreement on hearing that the task had been imposed by Eurystheus. This refusal afterwards led to a war between Hercules and Elis.

7. The Cretan bull had been presented by Poseidon to Minos, and by him placed among the herd of cattle sacred to the sun. How it became wild, and how Pasiphae, the wife of Minos, conceiving a passion for it, followed it over the island, has been told in connection with the legends of Crete. The task imposed on Hercules was to bring this bull to Mykense. The first difficulty was to capture and subdue it, an act in which he is frequently represented on the painted vases. The second was to bring it over the sea to Mykenae, which he did by sitting on its back while it swam, as did Europa with Zeus, in the shape of a bull. As to the fate of the bull, it is said that Eurystheus sacrificed it to Hera, and, again, that it escaped, roved wildly over the Peloponnesus, and was finally captured at

Marathon by Theseus.

8. The horses of Diomedes, a king of Thrace, and reputed to have been a son of Ares, the god of war and the personification of storm. Like the people whom he ruled, Diomedes was fierce in war. His seat was in the neighborhood of Abdera, where in later times the remains of his citadel was pointed out. He was the owner of certain horses which fed on human flesh, and by that means became furious and so powerful that they had to be fastened with iron chains. The human flesh on which they fed was generally that of persons who had been wrecked on that inhospitable coast. Hercules was ordered to bring these horses to Mykense. To Abdera he went by sea; and on arriving overpowered the guards, and led the horses away to the shore, when he was overtaken by a crowd of the subjects of Diomedes. A terrible fight ensued, in which the king fell at the hands of Hercules, and was himself given as food for his horses. In the course of the combat, Abderos, a beautiful youth, of whom Hercules was very fond, fell; and in his honor the hero raised a mound, and instituted games in his honor, which the people of Abdera afterwards continued annually. After the horses had been conveyed to Mykense and presented to Eurystheus, it is said that they escaped among the hills of Arcadia, and were there ultimately devoured by wild beasts — probably by the wolves of Zeus Lykaeos. Their allegorical signification is clearly that of storms and billows, and hence the legend was located in Thrace, a country with which we are familiar in connection

with other personifications of storm — such as Ares, Lykurgos, and Boreas.

9. The girdle of Hippolyte, the queen of the Amazons, had been a gift from Ares, and was a symbol of the power of a rushing headlong storm. The task imposed on Hercules was to fetch this girdle for Admete, the daughter of Eurystheus, of whom we learn elsewhere that she was a priestess of the Argive Hera. Hercules slew the Amazon, and returned with the girdle. From this adventure appears to have arisen the legend of a war conducted by Hercules against the Amazons.

1 o. The cattle of Geryon or Geryoneus, who was a son of Chrysaor and the Okeanide nymph Kallirrhoe. He was quite a sight – in one person he had three bodies, three heads, three pairs of legs, and six arms. He was gigantic in size, heavily armed, powerful, and provided with wings. The great point of his character was that he was the lord of immense herds of cattle. Considering that the possession of herds of cattle was also a prominent feature in the character of Apollo and Helios, in whose case the cattle represented the days of the year, and considering further that the local habitation of Geryon, though assigned to various localities, is always assigned to a place in some way connected with the worship of Helios, it may be inferred that Geryon also was an illustration of some of the phenomena of the sky; and of these phenomena none but those of wintry storms correspond with his personal appearance and vehemence. Geryon keeps his cattle at night in a dark cave in the

remote west, into which Hercules penetrates, and drives them away eastward towards the region of morning light.

The expedition had three stages: first, the journey to Erytheia, where Geryon lived, and which, judged by the meaning of its name, seems to be connected with the red glow of sunset; secondly, the contest with Geryon; and, thirdly, the return to Mykense with the cattle. Erytheia was an island somewhere in the remote west, beyond the pillars of Hercules; and to reach it the hero employed a vessel, obtained, some said, from Nereus, while others believed that he had compelled Helios to lend him for the occasion the cup or vessel in which he was accustomed to sail every night round the world from west to east. On the passage Hercules was alarmed, or at any rate disturbed, by a storm, which was only appeased by his drawing his bow on Okeanos. Reaching the island, he placed himself on Mount Abas, but was observed by the two- headed dog of Geryon, and attacked by it. He slew the dog, and was next attacked by the herdsman Eurytion, who also fell at his hands.

Then Menoitios, who was there watching the cattle of Helios, pointed out to him the cattle of Geryon, grazing in a meadow by the river's side. He was in the act of driving them away, when Geryon himself, in all his strength and fierceness, appeared on the scene. The combat was ended by a fatal shaft from Hercules. Shipping the cattle into the vessel of the sun, and landing them safely, Hercules commenced his homeward journey on foot, through Iberia, Gaul, over the Alps, and down through Italy, with many adventures, in all of which he was successful. At Rome occurred the incident with the robber Cacous, which the Romans incorporated among their national legends, though the elements of it were obviously of a Greek origin.

At the Phlegroean fields, near Cumae, he fought the Giants. On the mountains between Rhegium and Locri, his rest was disturbed by the noise of the grasshoppers, and at his prayer the gods removed these creatures from the district forever. From the south of Italy one of his bulls escaped across the sea to Sicily, and as it was necessary to follow it, Hercules, holding on by the horns of another bull, crossed with his herd to that island, through the length and breadth of which he appears to have wandered, encountering giants like Eryx, experiencing kindness from the nymphs of Himera and Egesta, at whose warm springs he was refreshed, and everywhere leaving reminiscences of his visit. Thence he passed up the shores of the Adriatic, round by Illyria and Epirus to Ambracia, where a gadfly, sent by Hera, caused his cattle to run away in great numbers to the mountains. With the remainder he reached the Hellespont, and thence proceeded to Mykense, where Eurystheus sacrificed them to the goddess Hera.

11. The apples of the Hesperides. According to later story, the last labor imposed on Hercules was to procure three of the golden apples which grew in the garden of the Hesperides; and hence

in works of art which represent him as invictus, the invincible, he appears holding the apples in his hand. As in the case of the cattle of Geryon, here also the chief interest of the legend resides in the adventures on the way. As regards the locality where this wonderful garden was to be found, there was a difference of opinion; some, apparently under the influence of Phoenician traditions, believing it to have been in the remote west, while Eschylos and others conceived that Atlas and the Hesperides lived in the northern region of the Hyperboreans. From the combination of both beliefs in later times, a very wide scope was given to the adventures of the hero on his way there and back.

Hercules himself, not knowing what direction to take, is said to have first passed through Macedonia and on to the Rhone, where he met certain nymphs who advised him that Nereus, the sea-god, knew the secret, and could be made to give it up. In spite of the many transformations of Nereus, Hercules compelled him to tell him the way. He then proceeded to Libya, where he found Antseos, a giant of enormous strength, whose habit was to kill all travelers who crossed the waste where he lived. He was a son of Poseidon and the Earth, deriving from his mother a strength that rendered him invincible to those who could not lift him from the ground, which Hercules did.

The wrestling scene between the two was a favorite subject in ancient art, and commended itself largely to the Greek youths as they practiced in the palaestra. When he had conquered Antseos, Hercules lay down to rest, and in a little while found himself covered with a host of creatures called Pygmies, who sprang up from the waste. He wrapped them in his lion's skin and killed them. From Libya he went into Egypt, where he was seized by the orders of Busiris and conveyed, as were all strangers, to be sacrificed. He burst his bonds, and offered up instead Busiris, his son, and retinue. From Egypt he went to India, and thence returned in a northerly direction towards the Caucasus mountains, where he set free Prometheus, and in return for that kindly act was told the way on through Scythia to the region of the Hyperboreans, where lived Atlas and the Hesperides. Part of the arrangement was that Atlas should pluck the three apples for him; and to relieve him for that purpose it was necessary that Hercules should take the burden of the world on his shoulders. Atlas returned with the apples, and naively proposed that he himself should convey them to Eurystheus. Hercules appeared to appreciate the proposal, and only wished first to find a pad to save his head from the weight. Atlas did not see the joke, and willingly took the world on his shoulders again. Hercules, of course, did not return. Another report has it that Hercules himself entered the garden, slew the dragon that watched the tree, and carried off the apples and returned with them to Eurystheus.

12. Cerberus, the three-headed dog of Hades, which guarded the entrance to the lower world, was a symbol of the eternal darkness of Hades.

The task of bringing it to the upper world was regarded in the earlier epic poetry as the most difficult of the labors of Hercules. It was supposed that he entered from the upper world through a chasm near Taenarum, returning by the same way. The shades of the dead fled in terror when they beheld him. Near the gates he found his friends Theseus and Peirithoos seated on a rock, to which they were attached as if they had grown from it, and in great trouble. He freed Theseus, but the earth shook when he tried to do the same for Peirithoos. To impart life to the shades of his friends whom he freed, he obtained blood from one of the cows of Hades, which he killed after a severe fight with Menoites, the herdsman.

Hercules did the impossible and overcame every obstacle that the gods capriciously threw at him. At last he reached Pluto, who agreed that he might take Cerberus provided he could do so without the assistance of arms of any kind. This he succeeded in doing, and leading the hated dog to Eurystheus, completed his twelve labors.

The Hunt of the Calydonian Boar

This famous boar was a mythical monster sent by Artemis to attack Calydon out of revenge. The king of this region earned her wrath because did not properly honor the divine huntress as he was paying due respects to the other gods in a ceremony. The creature was so fearsome that it took all the heroes of the new age to vanquish it, sans Hercules who was busy fighting the

Erymanthian boar.

At the head of this expedition was Meleagros, a son of Ceneus, the king of Calydon, and his wife Althaea; Deianeira, the wife of Hercules, being a daughter of the same pair. At the birth of Meleagros the Parcae appeared to Althaea, and Atropos told her that her infant would live as long as a brand which she pointed to on the fire remained unconsumed. Althaea snatched it that moment from the flames, hid it away carefully, and thus secured the invulnerability of the newborn Meleagros. On growing to manhood he took part in the Argonautic expedition, and is said to have signalized himself by many acts of bravery; but the enterprise with which his fame was most associated was the successful hunt of the ferocious boar, that was laying waste the country round Calydon, defying the spears and hounds of ordinary huntsmen.

The hunting party was quite impressive. Meleagros sent messengers round Greece to invite all its bravest heroes to Calydon to join him in the hunt. There came Idas and Lynkeus from Messene, Kastor and Polydeukes (Pollux) from Lakedaemon, Theseus from Athens, Admetos from Pherse, Ankaeos and the beautiful Atalante from Arcadia, Jason from Iolkos, Peleus from Thessaly, and many other well-proved heroes. After enjoying for nine days, as was usual, the hospitality of Meleagros, they prepared on the tenth for the chase, which, with a few accidents, resulted in the death of the boar by the spear of Meleagros, to whom accordingly fell the trophy of the monster's head and skin.

As, however, Atalante had been the first to wound the boar, Meleagros made that a pretext for presenting her with its skin. But on her way homewards to Arcadia she was met and forcibly robbed of it by the brothers of Althaea, the mother of Meleagros, who considered that they had a superior claim to that part of the booty. A quarrel arose on that account between Meleagros and his uncles; they fought, and the end of it was that the uncles were slain. To avenge their death, Althaea cast the brand, which up till then she had carefully preserved, into the fire, and thereupon her brave son was seized with dreadful pain, and died. Grief at the rashness of her act caused the mother to kill herself. Artemis, it appears, got the last laught.

The Expedition of the Argonauts

The famous story of Jason and the Argonauts is at its core one of inter-rivalry among the gods and direct assistance given by them so that they may score points against their enemies. Hera directly intervened in a rivalry between Jason and King Pelias over the latter ignoring the goddess in favor of Poseidon. To understand the object of this expedition, it will be necessary to go back a little into the genealogy of the person at whose instance it was conducted. That person was Jason, a son of Jeson, the rightful king of Iolkos in Thessaly, and his wife Alkimede. The father of Eson was Eolos (a son of Hellen and a grandson of Deukalion), at whose death he succeeded to the throne, but was driven from it by Pelias, his stepbrother, at whose hands he and all his relatives suffered cruel persecution.

The boy Jason was saved from harm by some of his father's friends, and placed under the care and instruction of the Centaur Cheiron. At the age of twenty he was told by an oracle to present himself to Pelias, and claim his father's kingdom. Pelias also had learned from the oracle that a descendant of Eolos would dethrone him, and, moreover, that the descendant in question would appear to him for the first time with only one sandal to his feet. Pelias, the usurper, was therefore anxiously looking out for the approach of a person in this plight. It happened that the river Enipeus was swollen when Jason reached it, on his way to put forth his claim against Pelias. But Hera, the patron goddess of Iolkos, taking the form of an old woman, conveyed him across, with no loss except that of one sandal. Jason would soon learn the blessing of helping an old woman cross the river.

On his arrival at Iolkos, Pelias recognized him as the rightful heir referred to by the oracle, but, at the same time, was unwilling to abdicate in his favor. He would prefer that Jason should first do something in the way of heroic enterprise, and, as a suitable adventure of that kind, proposed that he should fetch the golden fleece from Kolchis. Jason agreed to this, and set about building the Argo, the largest ship that had as yet sailed from Greece. The goddess Athena aided him with her skill and advice in the work, as did also Hera. When the ship was ready, Jason sent messengers to invite the foremost heroes of

Greece to join him in his enterprise. Among the many who accepted his invitation were Hercules, Kastor and Pollux, Meleagros, Orpheus, Peleus, Neleus, Admetos, Theseus, his friend Peirithoos, and the two sons of Boreas, Kalai's and Zetes.

We now come to the story of the golden fleece, which in order to understand properly requires a brief digression into the family feuding of Jason's line. We must go back to Eolos, whom we have mentioned above as grandfather of Jason and son of Helen. This Eolos had, besides Alson, another son, Athamas, who married Nephele, and had two children, Phrixos and Helle. On the death of his wife, Athamas married a second time Ino, a daughter of Kadmos, by whom he had two sons, Learchos and Melikertes. The second wife disliking her two stepchildren, made several attempts on their lives. To save them from further danger, the shade of their mother, it was said, appeared to Phrixos, bringing at the same time a large ram with a golden fleece, on which she proposed Phrixos and Helle should escape over the sea. They started according to her advice, and Phrixos reached safely the opposite shore, but Helle fell from the ram's back into the sea and was drowned. The name of Hellespont was in consequence given to the strait that they had to cross. Phrixos, having reached the other side, proceeded to Kolchis, on the farthest shore of the Black Sea, and there sacrificed the ram to Zeus, in honor of his safety. He hung the golden fleece up in the temple of Ares.

Previous to starting from Iolkos, Jason

offered a sacrifice to Zeus, calling upon the god for a sign of his favor, or displeasure if it should be so. Zeus answered with thunder and lightning, which was taken as a favorable omen. The expedition proceeded first to Lemnos, where the heroes were kindly received, remained a long time, and – taking an appropriate length of time to be fruitful and multiply – became the fathers of a new race of heroes. The women of the island had, it would seem, at the instigation of Aphrodite, slain their husbands. One of the Lemnian women, Hypsipyle, bore a son to Jason, and called him Euneos. Leaving Lemnos and its festive life, the Argonauts continued their journey as far as Kyzikos, where they landed for a short time, and were in the act of leaving, when Hercules, having broken his oar, left the ship, accompanied by Hylas, to cut a new oar in the wood. But some nymphs, admiring the beauty of young Hylas, carried him off; and as Hercules would not leave the country without him, the expedition was compelled to proceed without the assistance and companionship of the great hero.

Their next landing was in the neighborhood of the modern Scutari, where the reigning king, Amykos, was famed as a boxer. Like many boxers, he had a destructive personality and was also know for his cruelty to all strangers who entered his territories. Seeing the Argonauts land for the purpose of obtaining fresh water, he sent them, as was his custom, a challenge to match him with a boxer, which Pollux accepted, and proved the skill by which he earned his fame upon the boastful Amykos. Proceeding on their journey, they passed through the perilous entrance to the Black Sea in safety, owing their escape from its dangers to the advice of Phineus, the blind and aged king of the district, whom they had found suffering great distress on account of his food being always carried off or polluted by the Harpys, just as he sat down to eat it. This punishment, as well as his blindness, had been sent upon him by the gods in consequence of his cruelty to his wife (a daughter of Boreas) and children. The Harpys were driven away effectually by the two sons of Boreas, who accompanied the Argonauts; and it was in return for this kindness that Phineus communicated his plan for a safe passage through the Symplegades, two great cliffs that moved upon their bases, and crushed everything that ventured to pass between. His plan was first to fly a pigeon through between them, and then the moment that the cliffs, having closed upon the pigeon, began to move to each side, to row the Argo swiftly through the passage. It was done, and before the cliffs could close upon her, the ship, all but her rudder, had got clear of danger. From that time the Symplegades were united into one rock.

After many other adventures the expedition at last reached Kolchis, where they found Eetes, a reputed son of Helios and Persei's, reigning as king. He refused to give up the golden fleece, except to the man who should acquit himself to his satisfaction in certain enterprises which he proposed. The first was to yoke to a plough his unmanageable bulls, that snorted fire and had hoofs of brass, and to plough, the field of Ares with them. That done, the field was to be sown with a dragon's teeth, from which armed men were to spring in the furrows. The hero who succeeded so far was then to be permitted to fetch, if he could, the golden fleece, which hung on an oak in a grove sacred to Ares, and was watched continually by a monstrous dragon. Jason, ever the charmer, was able to accomplish these tasks by winning the affection of Medea, the daughter of Eetes. She prepared him for these dangerous tasks by means of a witch's mixture which made him proof against fire and sword. The goddess Athena also helped him, and his success was complete.

The Argonauts now commenced their homeward voyage, Jason taking with him Medea. On missing his daughter, Eetes gave pursuit. Seeing that he was overtaking them, Medea, to divert his course, decided to do the most irrational thing imaginable and dismembered her young brother, Absyrtos, whom she had taken with her, and cast the limbs about in the sea. The delay caused to Eetes in collecting the pieces of his child, enabled Medea and Jason to escape. According to another report, Absyrtos had by that time grown to manhood, and met his death in an encounter with Jason, in pursuit of whom he had been sent by his father.

After passing through many other dangers, Jason at last reached Iolkos, and, presenting the golden fleece to Pelias, claimed the throne, as agreed upon. But Pelias still refused to abdicate.

Jason therefore slew him, and assumed the government of Iolkos, together with that of Corinth, where Jeetes, the father of Medea, had, it is said, ruled before he went to Kolchis.

Ten years of peace followed the accession of Jason to the throne. The origin of the troubles that fell upon the royal house thereafter was an attachment formed by Jason for the beautiful Kreusa, whom he made his wife in Corinth. Jason's mistake was to jilt a women well versed in sorcery. Medea, stung with jealousy, turned to the arts of witchcraft she had learned in Kolchis, and having steeped a dress and a costly wreath in poison, sent them to her rival, and by that means caused her death. Not content with that, she set fire to the palace of Kreon, the father of Kreusa; and further, finding Jason enraged at what she had done, she put to death the children she herself had borne to him, and fled to Athens, where, as we have seen, she lived for a time with Egeus. Thence also she had to escape, in consequence of an attempt on the life of Theseus. She went back to Kolchis, some believed, in a chariot drawn by winged dragons.

Jason, it is said, depressed by his troubles, repaired to the sanctuary on the Isthmus of Corinth, where the Argo had been consecrated in the grove of Poseidon. On approaching the ship, part of the stern gave way, fell upon him, and caused his death. Another version of the story says that he took his own life.

The Trojan War

No discussion of the petty behavior of the gods and their insertion into the affairs of man is complete without a discussion of the most epic battle in history. Homer's "The Iliad" is many things, but it is clearly a story of the gods taking sides between the Greeks and Trojans, and advancing or sacrificing heroes in this story like pieces on a chess board. The unfortunate pawns found themselves destroyed when they impeded a strategy of the gods, but the fortunate knights or queens became characters of unimaginable renown in ancient Greece.

The story began with an argument between Aphrodite, Hera, and Athena. Eris, the goddess of strife, gave to them the Apple of Discord, which could not have led to anything resembling non-violent conflict resolution. The apple was to be given to the fairest, and the three goddesses decided to allow the Trojan prince Paris to decide the winner in the celestial beauty contest. Clearly Aphrodite had an unfair advantage, and she was chosen as the winner. As a reward to Paris she made Helen, judged to be the most beautiful women on earth and the wife of Menelaus, fall in love with him. She ran off with Paris to Troy, and this cuckolding gave Agamemnon, Menelaus's brother, a reasonable excuse to launch an invasion of Troy. They would come to besiege the city for ten years, and these events started a chain reaction that mostly led to the destruction of Troy and scattering of the Greeks, along with severe infighting among gods and men due to a tangled web of alliances that made World War I appear straightforward by comparison.

The First Years of the War.

The Trojans having received intelligence of the hostile preparations of the Greeks, prepared on their part also to meet the enemy, assembling in and around the city of Troy all the forces they could obtain from neighbors and allies. Their foremost hero, whom they chose to lead them in assaults, was Hector, the eldest son of the king. The first engagement of the two forces occurred while the Greeks were in the act of landing from their ships, the result of it being that the Trojans were driven back within their walls, but not without inflicting considerable loss on their enemy. The first attempt of the Greeks to take the town by storm entirely failed, and, finding that the Trojans would not surrender Helen to her husband, the Greek commander could see no other means of compelling them to do so than by a siege. Accordingly a well-fortified camp was constructed round the ships, which had been hauled up on the shore, and with that camp to fall back upon, the Greek army proceeded to lay waste the territory and towns in the neighborhood. The Trojan forces, acknowledging the superiority of the besiegers, did not seek a battle, and excepting such incidents as when Achilles and Hector fought in single combat, or when Troilos, the youngest son of Priam, was captured and put to death by Achilles, nothing of moment transpired.

In the course of the raids made by the Greeks in the neighborhood, it happened that having taken the town of Pedasos, and come to divide the spoils, Agamemnon obtained as his captive Chryseis, a daughter of Chryses, the priest of Apollo in the island of Chryse, while to the lot of Achilles fell Briseis, a maiden as beautiful as the priest's daughter. Chryses entreated Agamemnon to restore him his daughter, offering a heavy ransom for her, but was met with refusal and contumely. Having one other resource — an appeal to the god in whose service he was — Chryses implored the aid of Apollo, who, being for other reasons also hostile to the Greeks, visited them with a plague which carried them off in great numbers. This was one of the first acts of the gods directly intervening in the war.

Agamemnon called a muster of the army, and inquired of the high priest, Kalchas, by what the angry god could be appeased. Kalchas, being assured of the protection of Achilles, boldly declared that the wrath of Apollo had been caused by the unjust detention of Chryseis, a daughter of one of his priests. Upon this, Agamemnon, who had borne a grudge against Kalchas ever since the sacrifice of Iphigeneia, rated the priest in reproachful terms, charging him also in the present instance with being in league with Achilles — a charge which the latter would have resented with force, had not the goddess Athena interposed. Agamemnon felt his dignity as king and commander of the army insulted by the threat of Achilles, and demanded as satisfaction for this the person of the beautiful Briseis, apparently to take the place of Chryseis, who he had been compelled to give up. Achilles having been warned by Athena to be calm, confessed his inability to resist the demand, and from that time withdrew with all his men from the camp.

Thetis having beseeched Zeus to take measures to compel Agamemnon to atone for this insult to her son, obtained a divine decree setting forth that so long as Achilles held aloof the Greeks would be defeated in every engagement with the Trojans. Emboldened by the intelligence of the step taken by Achilles, the Trojans sallied from their walls, and after numerous battles, skirmishes, and personal encounters, always attended with serious loss to the enemy, drove the Greeks back to the shelter of their fortified camp beside the ships. At last, abased and humiliated by disasters, Agamemnon sent an embassy to Achilles, offering to restore Briseis, and in addition to bestow on him his daughter's hand, with seven towns for a dowry. But the wrath of Achilles would not relent, and still the need of his countrymen grew worse.

The end seemed to be near when Hector, at the head of the Trojans, had stormed the wall of the camp, and set several of the ships on fire. Seeing this, Patroklos begged Achilles to lend him his armor, and allow him to lead the Myrmidons to the fight. The request being granted, Patroklos and his men were soon in the heat of the battle, their sudden reappearance striking the Trojan army with terror, and causing it to fall back. Not content with thus deciding the battle, Patroklos, disregarding the advice of Achilles, pursued the enemy till Hector, turning round, engaged him in a hand-to-hand fight, the issue of which was the death of the Greek hero. Hector stripped him of the armor of Achilles, which he wore, but left the body for the Greeks to take possession of.

The grief of Achilles at the loss of his friend was as violent as had been his anger against Agamemnon, and this act became the turning point of the war. He called for vengeance on Hector, and with the object in view of obtaining it, yielded to a reconciliation that all the sufferings of his countrymen could not previously induce him to submit to. With armor more dazzling and superb than had ever been seen before, forged by the god Hephsestos, and brought by Thetis in the hour of her son's need, he went forth to battle, seeking Hector in the Trojan ranks, which everywhere hurried back like sheep before a wolf. The Trojan hero stepped forth to meet his adversary, but not without sad misgivings. He had said farewell to his faithful wife, Andromache, and to his boy, Astyanax. But even the strong sense of duty to his country, which had supported him in this domestic scene, deserted him utterly when the young Greek hero approached with the dauntless bearing of the god of war himself. Hector fled; but Achilles, having a faster step, cut off his retreat, and thus imbued him with the courage of despair. The combat did not last long, the victory of Achilles being easily won.

Unappeased by the death of Hector, Achilles proceeded to outrage his lifeless body by binding it to his war-chariot. After dragging it thus three times round the walls of Troy in the face of the people, he returned with it to the Greek camp, and there cast it among dust and dirt. Displeased by such excess of passion, the gods took care of Hector's body, and saved it from corruption, while Zeus in the meantime softened the heart of Achilles, and prepared him for the performance of an act of generosity which was to blot out the memory of his previous cruelty. On the one hand, Thetis was employed to persuade her son to give up the body without a ransom.

On the other hand, Hermes was sent to bid Priam go stealthily in the night to Achilles' tent, and beg the body of his son. The aged king of Troy obeyed, and coming to the young hero's tent, besought him, as he valued his own father, to give him leave to take away the lifeless body, and pay to it the customary rites of burial. Achilles was touched by the gentleness of his beseeching, raised the old man from his knees, shared with him the hospitality of his tent, and, in the morning, having given up the body, sent him back under a safe escort. In the pause of hostilities that took place then, the Greeks buried the body of Patroklos with great ceremony.

The loss of Hector had so dispirited the Trojans, that without reinforcements they could not face the enemy again. Such reinforcements, however, consisting of an army of Amazons, under the command of the beautiful Penthesilea, arrived in the interval of mourning for Hector in the one camp and for Patroklos in the other. When hostilities commenced again, the valiant Penthesilea, being eager to measure her strength with that of Achilles, and to avenge the death of Hector, led the Trojan army into battle. The leaders of the Greeks were Achilles and Ajax, the son of Telamon. While the latter hero was engaged in driving back the Trojan ranks, Achilles and Penthesilea met in single combat. He would have spared her willingly, and did not, till compelled in self-defense, strike with all his might. Then she fell mortally wounded and as she fell, remembering the fate of Hector's body, implored Achilles to spare hers that disgrace. There was no need of this; for he, to save her still if possible, and if not, to soothe her last moments, lifted her in his arms, and there held her till she died. The Trojans and Amazons made a combined rush to rescue the body of their leader; but Achilles made a sign to them to halt, and praising her valor, youth, and beauty, gave it to them freely — a kindly act that touched friends and foes alike. Among the Greeks, however, there was one Thersites, mean and deformed in mind as well as body, who not only dared to impute a scandalous motive to Achilles, but, approaching the fallen Amazon, struck his spear into her lightless eye. A sudden blow from Achilles laid him lifeless on the ground.

All who saw this punishment inflicted approved of it, except Diomedes, the son of Tydeus, a relation by blood of Thersites, who stepped forward and demanded of Achilles the usual reparation, consisting of a sum of money. Feeling himself deeply wronged because his countrymen, and especially Agamemnon, did not unconditionally take his part in the matter,

Achilles abandoned for a second time the cause of the Greeks, and took ship to Lesbos. Odysseus was sent after him, and by dint of smooth words, cleverly directed, succeeded in bringing him back to the camp.

What made the return of Achilles more urgent at that time was the arrival of a new ally to the Trojans, in the person of Memnon, a son of Eos, and Tithonos, who besides being the son of a goddess, as well as Achilles, appeared further to be a proper match for him, inasmuch as he also carried armor fashioned by Hephestos. When the two heroes met, and were fighting fiercely, Zeus received in Olympos a simultaneous visit from their respective mothers,

Thetis and Eos, both imploring him to spare their sons. He answered that the issue must abide the will of Fate, Mcera, to discover which he took the golden balance for weighing out life and death, and placing in one scale the fate of Achilles and in the other that of Memnon, saw the latter sink to denote his death. Eos made haste to the battle-field, but found her son dead. She carried away his body, and buried it in his native land, in the distant east.

The Death of Achilles

The Greek hero did not have a chance to savor his victory due to another round of the gods intervening. Achilles did not long enjoy his triumph; for, animated by success, he led on the Greeks, and would have captured Troy, however clearly the Fates might have decreed the contrary, had not Apollo given unerring flight to an arrow drawn by Paris. By that shaft from an unworthy source, as far as could be judged, Achilles fell. Ajax, the stout hero, and Odysseus, clever as well as brave, seized his body, and fighting all the way, carried it back to the camp, where its burial was attended with extraordinary pomp and ceremonial, the Muses chanting dolorous lays, and the heroes who had known him personally taking part, as was the custom on such occasions, in athletic competitions. The armor which he had worn in the fight was offered by Thetis to the most deserving. Only two claims were preferred, and those were on behalf of the two heroes who had rescued his body. The award being given in favor of Odysseus, Ajax, from grief at what he deemed neglect, sank into a state of insanity, in the course of which he intentionally fell upon his sword, and died.

A cessation of hostilities was obtained on the death of Achilles and Ajax, the two foremost of the Greek heroes. This period of peace having expired, and the former conditions of war having been resumed, the first event of importance that occurred was the capture of Helenos, a son of Priam, who, like his sister, Kassandra, was endowed with the gift of prophecy. Odysseus, who had made the capture, compelled Helenos to disclose the measures by which it was decreed that the siege should be brought to a determination. The answer was, that to take the city of Troy, and thus close the siege, three things were necessary: 1, the assistance of the son of Achilles, Neoptolemos; 2, the bow and arrows of Hercules; 3, the possession of the Palladium (an image of the goddess Pallas-Athena), which was carefully preserved in the citadel of Troy. In satisfying the first condition no difficulty was experienced. Odysseus, always ready to be of service for the common good, proceeded to Skyros, where he found Neoptolemos grown to manhood, and thirsting for martial renown. A present of the splendid armor which his father, Achilles, had worn, and which Odysseus now magnanimously parted with, fired the youth's ambition, and led him easily to Troy, where he distinguished himself in a combat with Eurypylos (a son of Telephos), who had joined the Trojan ranks.

A more serious matter was the fulfillment of the second condition, seeing that the bow and arrows of Hercules were then in the possession of Philoktetes, whom, as we have already said, the Greeks abandoned at Lemnos, not caring to endure the screams caused by the wound in his foot. His feelings were known to be rancorous towards the Greeks. Notwithstanding that, Odysseus, accompanied by Diomedes (or, as others say, by Neoptolemos), went to Lemnos, and successfully tricked Philoktetes into following him to Troy, where his wound was healed by Machaeon, a son of Asklepios, and a reconciliation was effected between him and Agamemnon. The first on whom his fatal arrows were tried was Paris, after whose death Helena married his brother, Deiphobos. The Trojans were now completely shut up within the town, no one daring to face the arrows of Philoktetes.

There, remained, however, a third condition — the seizure of the Palladium. Odysseus, successful in the other two, and undaunted by the greater difficulty of the new adventure, proposed to steal alone within the walls of Troy in the disguise of a beggar, and as a first measure to find out where the Palladium was preserved. He did so, and remained unrecognized except by Helena, who, having felt ever since the death of Paris a yearning for Menelaos, proved to be a valuable ally. Odysseus, in the meantime, returned to the Greek camp to obtain the assistance of Diomedes. The two having made their way back to Troy, laid hold of the Palladium, and, carrying it off in safety, fulfilled the third and last condition.

The next difficulty was the plan of assault to be adopted. It was proposed by Odysseus, on the suggestion of the goddess Athena, that Epeios, a famous sculptor, should make a great wooden horse, sufficiently large to hold inside a number of the bravest Greeks, and that the horse being ready, and the heroes concealed within it beyond detection, the whole Greek army should embark and set sail, as if making homeward. The plan of Odysseus was agreed to, and great was the joy of the Trojans when they saw the fleet set sail. The people, scarcely trusting their eyes, flocked to the abandoned camp, to make sure. There they found nothing remaining but a great wooden horse, about the use of which various opinions arose — some thinking it an engine of war, and demanding its instant destruction. But the opinion that prevailed most was that it must have been an object of religious veneration, and if so, ought to be taken into the city. Among those who thought otherwise was Laokoon, a priest of Apollo, who had arrived on the scene, accompanied by his two young sons, to offer a sacrifice to the god in whose service he was. Laokoon warned his countrymen in no case to accept this gift of the Greeks, and went so far as to thrust his spear into the belly of the horse, upon which the weapons of the heroes within were heard to clash, and the bystanders were all but convinced of the justice of the priest's opinion. But the gods had willed it otherwise, and to turn the opinion of the people against Laokoon, sent a judgment upon him in the shape of two enormous serpents, which, while he and his two sons were engaged in sacrificing at an altar by the shore, issued from the sea, and casting their coils round the two boys first, then round the father, who came to their assistance, caused him to die in great agony.

But to carry out effectually the stratagem of the horse, Odysseus had left behind on the shore his friend Sinon, with his hands bound, and presenting all the appearance of a victim who had escaped sacrifice, which he professed to be. The good king Priam was touched by the piteous story that Sinon told, ordered his bonds to be struck off, and inquired the purpose of the horse. Sinon replied that it was a sacred object, and would, if taken into the city, be a guarantee of the protection of the gods, as the Palladium had been before. The city gates being too small, part of the wall was broken through, and the horse conducted in triumph towards the citadel. This done, the Trojans, believing that the Greeks had abandoned the siege in despair, gave way to festivity and general rejoicing, which lasted well into the night.

When the town had become perfectly quiet, the inhabitants, exhausted by the unusual excitement, being fast asleep, Sinon approached the horse, and opened a secret door in its side. The heroes then stepped out, and made a fire signal to the fleet, which lay concealed behind the neighboring island of Tenedos, and now advanced quietly to the shore. The troops having disembarked and made their way silently to the city, there ensued a fearful slaughter, the surprised inhabitants falling thickly before the well-armed Greeks. Finally the town was set on fire in every corner, and utterly destroyed. Priam fell by the hand of Neoptolemos. The same fate befell the son of Hector — not for anything that, he had done, but that he might not grow up to avenge his father's death. Of the few Trojans who escaped were Eneas, his father Anchises, and his infant son Askanios. Carrying his aged father on his shoulders, Eneas fled towards Mount Ida, and thence to Italy, where he became the founder of a new race.

Nearly all Trojans died in the conflict, and the Greeks were scattered. Odysseus and his men would take decades to return home, and his

stories are recounted in Homer's "The Odyssey."
As this story illustrates, when the gods became
involved in the affairs of men, mankind nearly
always suffered and the gods fared little better,
as all they gained was satisfaction for their egos,
which were rarely satiated for long.

Conclusion: When the Gods are Made in Our Image

This book has looked at the all-too-human character of the Greek gods and the way they made the human race, and themselves, suffer for their capricious actions. But are these stories merely quaint tales from a dead civilization or is there a modern lesson to impart even now? What do these stories mean for us today in the 21st century? Surprisingly, quite a bit.

Mythology is essentially the art of anthropomorphism – giving human personification to non-human subjects. The word, appropriately, is a portmanteau of the Greek words *anthropos* ("human being") and *morphe* ("shape"). Gods were given human bodies human emotions, such as love, envy, and hate. This stands in strong contrast to modern religions in which conceptions of God are understood to be transcendent to our human condition, and any discussion of God's "jealousy" or "envy" are purely metaphorical and only used as inferior words to provide us with a pale understanding of God's incommunicable attributes. The Greeks had no such hesitancy to paint their deities in such an unflattering light, and nobody elevated it to the level that the Greeks did, with their memorable stories, acts of heroism, and colorful characters that populated Mount Olympus.

There were two reasons that the Greeks used

anthropomorphism in their story telling. The first, as discussed in the introduction to this book, was that it was the most elegant way to understand the world around them. No science existed to explain natural phenomena such as weather patterns, the cause of earthquakes, or volcanic eruptions. Therefore it was reasonable to assume that just as a human ruler was responsible for laws and economic policy, a divine ruler was responsible for these natural events. Furthermore, believing that a personality caused these phenomena rather than random events ruled by chaos and uncertainty gave the ancient Greeks more control over their lives. If draught were unpredictable and irreversible then nihilism and fatalism would set in. But if ending the draught and bringing on a rainstorm only required displaying a proper level of sycophancy to the right god, then nature itself could be manipulated.

The second reason that Greeks used anthropomorphism in their story telling was that it was an effective way to disarm the audience and teach them truths about human nature. Somewhat ironically, humans could accept comments and critiques about humans if they thought the story was about someone else but not themselves. A man could laugh at the fickle nature of Hera without realizing that subconsciously he was laughing at women in general or his wife in particular. Likewise, women in society could hear about the less-than-savory exploits of Zeus that he committed behind Hera's back and the subterfuge committed by the male gods against each other and easily place the men in their lives in the same role. And all Greeks could make mention of the gods abusing their power and issue thinly-veiled insults against their own kings without worrying about receiving their wrath.

Yet over time ancient civilizations began to call into question the whole enterprise of worshiping such capricious beings that could bless them one minute and turn them into a cow the next. Developments in Greek philosophy and possibly the influence of the monotheistic Jewish neighbors encouraged intellectuals to begin scrubbing their religion of such crude elements. In the fifth century B.C. the philosopher Xenophanes commented on the anthropomorphic nature of religion – noticing that the Ethiopians to the south imagined their gods to be dark-skinned, while the Thracians to the north imagined them to be fair skinned and having red hair. He made a comment similar to Mark Twain's 19th century observation that God created man in his image and that many decided to return the favor. Socrates agreed with this sentiment, and two centuries later argued that man should not attribute his failings to the gods. It was precisely for this reason that the poets of Athens killed him, for he exposed their stories as myths that, while entertaining, were not suitable for moral instruction or philosophy to create a virtuous society.

Plato followed his instructor's lead and dug deeper into the questions of absolute moral standards. While he understood that pious activity pleased the gods, he did not accept a definition of piety that merely meant it was anything that happened to please the gods. This standard was too arbitrary and could not apply to all situations in the same way. If that were the case, then non-stop drunken revelry at a feast of Dionysus would be the height of piety (an idea that many Greeks would have likely found acceptable). He posed the question: are pious things pious because those things happen to please the gods or are the gods pleased by those things because they are pious and connect to a higher truth that is immutable and unchanging?

From this point Plato began to articulate the idea of an objective good and he came to his famous cave analogy – that the things we see and touch are only the physical reality, and there is an immaterial reality that contains perfect forms of all things. No god in his right mind, Plato argued, would lower himself into the physical world and debase himself, particularly by doing such things as taking on human form impregnating a human woman and then retreating back to Mount Olympus at the first signs of conception.

In the following decades Socrates's teachings were spread and expanded upon by Plato and Aristotle, and soon his teaching became the foundation of Greek education. While lip service to the gods continue for centuries into the Christian era, the intelligentsia of Greek and Roman society over time came to change their religious ideology. They started to see the gods as beings that, while not the standards of goodness and justice, had perfect knowledge of these attributes. And through wisdom humans could attain these virtues in increasing measure.

This was ultimately what did in the Greek gods. Their behavior became harder to whitewash and their apologists had to resort to more creative strategies to justify their brutish behavior. Society soon abandoned them for belief systems that could be better substantiated by philosophy. Philosophers later considered them not as creatures worthy of prayer, but as curiosities from an earlier time in history.

Long after their relevance had passed by, William Shakespeare considering the nature of the Greek gods. While his plays owed an enormous debt to ancient mythology, he thought quite little of the gods themselves. He wrote an unflattering description of them that many ancient Greeks likely thought, but were too afraid to voice for fear of divine repercussions: "As flies to wanton boys, are we to the gods; they kill us for their sport."

Excerpt from "History's Most Insane Rulers: Lunatics, Eccentrics, and Megalomaniacs

From Caligula to Kim Jong-Il"

Chapter 1:

Roman Emperor Caligula (r. 37-41 A.D.)

How to Lead by Appointing Your Horse Senator

When Salvador Dali set out to paint a depiction of the infamous Roman Emperor Caligula in 1971, he chose to depict the thing nearest and dearest to the crazed emperor's heart: his horse Incitatus. The painting "*Le Cheval de Caligula*" shows the pampered pony in all his royal glory. It is wearing an opulent crown and clothed in fine garments. While the gaudy clothing of the horse is historically correct, for once in his life the Spanish surrealist artist is guilty of severe understatement.

Emperor Caligula, who reigned from 37-41 A.D., was the first emperor with no memory of the pre-Augustan era and therefore had no compunction about establishing a personality cult, ruling with absolute autocracy, demanding his subjects' worship, and treating his horse better than royalty. According to the Roman historian Suetonius, he gave Incitatus 18 servants, a marble stable, an ivory manger, rich red robes, and a jeweled collar. He required that those passing by bow to his horse and demanded that it be fed oats mixed with flex of gold and wine delivered by fine goblets. Dignitaries were forced to tolerate the horse as a guest of honor at banquets. This episode was but one example of the deranged excesses to which Caligula lived and what led to his violent death at the hands of his enemies.

In the four short years that Gaius Julius Caesar Augustus Germanicus (Caligula) served as emperor of Rome, he built for himself a reputation as a man who was committed wholly to his lusts at the expense of his empire. He used his authority, influence and wealth to satisfy his sexual appetite, build his own ego and antagonize the Roman senate. Such behavior is thought to have been the primary reason he also went down in history as the first Roman emperor to be assassinated.

As the third child born to Germanicus (the legendary Roman general and adopted son of the emperor Tiberius) and grandson of the emperor Augustus on his mother's side, Gaius had grown up around Roman soldiers and powerful leaders. His youth was rife with difficulties. In 19 A.D., Caligula's father died under questionable circumstances, leaving his mother, Agrippina the Elder, to manage a strenuous relationship with the emperor Tiberius. Shortly after the death of his father, Caligula was sent to live with his great-grandmother, Livia. When she died two years later, he was sent to his grandmother, Antonia.

When the emperor Tiberius took ill and secluded himself on the island of Capri, he called for Caligula to be with him there on the island. In 31 A.D., Caligula accepted the invitation and went to tend to his adoptive grandfather. During that time, emperor Tiberius ordered the exile of Caligula's mother and two brothers. They later died, leaving Caligula as the sole male heir of Germanicus.

It is said that even in his illness, Tiberius could tell that Caligula, whom he had appointed joint successor along with his grandson, Tiberius Gemmellus, was not suitable to reign. The emperor referred to him as a viper that he thought would be unleashed on all of Rome. So Caligula was assigned only menial tasks and held no major offices between 31 and 37 A.D. When Tiberius died in 37 A.D., the Roman people received their new emperor with open arms, largely based on the fact that his father, Germanicus, had been so popular and well-loved. They were hopeful for a ruler who would demonstrate more warmth and charity than had Tiberius, who was notably isolated and stingy during his decades-long reign.

The beginning of Caligula's rule went well. He was a strong leader -- compassionate, smart and decisive. His first order of business was to pay off all of the former emperor's debts. He also honored his slain family by retrieving their remains and giving them a proper Roman burial. He gave the Praetorian guard a handsome bonus, recalled all exiles, and compensated those whom he thought had been wrongly taxed.

Not long into his reign, however, he fell ill and is said to have slipped into a coma. When he awoke, he was a very different man. Caligula had Tiberius Gemmellus killed and began to pursue the sexual appetite he had for his female siblings. He particularly liked his sister, Drusilla, whom he later married and impregnated. Not only did he have conjugal relations with them but he also prostituted them out to other men, effectively turning the palace into a brothel. After Drusilla's death, Caligula married twice more. Both marriages were short-lived. In 38 A.D., just one year after taking office, he married a fourth time to Milonia Caeconia.

Caligula was not at all concerned about the expansion of his empire, nor did he allocate any resources to defeating enemies. In just a few months, he managed to waste the entire fortune left by the emperor Tiberius, a fortune it had taken the former emperor 22 years to collect in tribute. In an effort to increase the amount of money available for his personal use, Caligula ordered all wealthy citizens to name him as the sole heir to their estates upon their deaths. Once that law was in place, he then began a campaign of falsely accusing, fining and killing wealthy citizens to get their money. He also tried and killed his wealthiest subjects for treason on charges of blasphemy so that he might receive their estates. He levied taxes on everything from marriage to prostitution and caused starvation in parts of his empire by claiming large areas of arable land for his own private use. He auctioned the lives of gladiators and claimed the plunder that soldiers had acquired from spoils during war.

Despite the fact that he quickly depleted the treasury and began heavily taxing his subjects, Caligula embarked on several vanity construction projects. He wanted a giant floating bridge built across the Bay of Baiae (Naples) in order to prove wrong the astrologer Trasyllus, who said that "Caligula had no more chance of becoming emperor than of crossing the bay of Baiae on horseback." According to the Roman historian Suetonius he crafted a solution by doing the following:

"He devised a novel and unheard of kind of pageant; for he bridged the gap between Baiae and the mole at Puteoli, a distance of about thirty-six hundred paces, by bringing together merchant ships from all sides and anchoring them in a double line, after which a mound of earth was heaped upon them and fashioned in the manner of the Appian Way. Over this bridge he rode back and forth for two successive days attended by the entire Praetorian guard and a company of his friends in Gallic chariots."

As he rode back and forth on horseback, Caligula made sure to wear the breastplate of Alexander the Great to shore up his military bona fides. He never actually attempted to go to war, but he did commission the construction of two large war ships that eventually burned without ever having been sailed. The closest he came was in 39-40 A.D. when he went to Gaul and marched to the shores with the military with the intent of invading Britain. Before his army launched its attack, he ordered them to stop and collect seashells. He called these the "spoils of the conquered ocean" and ordered his troops home.

Caligula was perpetually disrespectful of the Senate, who, during the reign of Tiberius had done much of the decision-making on their own, as Tiberius was quite anti-social. In response to their disapproval of him, Caligula did what he could to shame, embarrass and humiliate senate members, both individually and collectively. One famous incident involved his beloved horse, Incatitus, whom Caligula clothed in the finest robes, suitable for most any member of the nobility. Often times when invitations were sent from the palace, they were in the horse's name, and Incatitus was allowed to eat dinner at the emperor's table . It was also said by some Roman historians that Caligula attempted to make Incatitus either a senator or a priest before the emperor's death.

Caligula fully embraced emperor worship and encouraged others to worship him as a god. While previous emperors tolerated this practice, he allowed it and attempted to require it in the Roman provinces. Caligula tried to construct a huge statue of himself inside the Temple in Jerusalem, the center of Jewish worship. This action would have nearly guaranteed a revolt from the Jews, who would have considered the construction a pagan slap to the face of their religion. Herod Agrippa, the descendant of the man who slaughtered dozens of infants in an attempt to kill Jesus, even considered this a terrible idea and convinced the emperor to relent.

It was this consistent and unrelenting disrespect that eventually led to his murder. In early 41 A.D., in a secluded hall in the basement of the palace, Caligula was stabbed 30 times in an attack led by Cassius Chaerea, a guard whom Caligula had humiliated on multiple occasions. The painful and bloody attack didn't kill the emperor right away. But by the time his guards found him, the conspirators were long gone, and he eventually succumbed to his injuries. His wife Caeconia and their infant child were murdered as well.

Few sources contemporary with his life have survived, and his legacy is a bit open to embellishment. Nevertheless, nearly all historians agree that his cruel temperament and extravagance defined him as an emperor. They made for a legacy that far surpassed any positive contributions he gave to Rome.

[End of Excerpt] If you enjoy this portion of "History's Most Insane Rulers: Lunatics, Eccentrics, and Megalomaniacs From Caligula to Kim Jong-Il" you can grab your copy on Amazon.com.

Connect With Michael

I hope you have enjoyed this e-book and learned much about the oh-so-human nature of classical mythology.

You can connect with me on my homepage at http://michaelrank.net. Here you can find podcasts, blog posts, free book promotions, and other bits about history.

About the Author

Michael Rank is a doctoral candidate in Middle East history. He has studied Turkish, Arabic, Persian, Armenian, and French but can still pull out a backwater Midwestern accent if need be. He also worked as a journalist in Istanbul for nearly a decade and reported on religion and human rights.

He is the author of the #1 Amazon best-seller "From Muhammed to Burj Khalifa: A Crash Course in 2,000 Years of Middle East History," and "History's Most Insane Rulers: Lunatics, Eccentrics, and Megalomaniacs From Emperor Caligula to Kim Jong Il."

One Last Thing

If you enjoyed this book, I would be grateful if you leave a review on Amazon. Your feedback allows me to improve current and future projects.

Thank you again for your support!

Made in United States
North Haven, CT
18 August 2024

56256173R00085